MISSING

... AND PRESUMED DEAD

A TRUE STORY BY

MICHAEL FLEEMAN

WILD BLUE
PRESS

WildBluePress.com

MISSING ... AND PRESUMED DEAD published by:
WILDBLUE PRESS
P.O. Box 102440
Denver, Colorado 80250

WILDBLUE PRESS is registered at the U.S. Patent and Trademark Offices.

ISBN 978-1-948239-96-7   Trade Paperback
ISBN 978-1-948239-97-4   eBook

Interior Formatting/Book Cover Design by Elijah Toten
www.totencreative.com

MISSING
... AND PRESUMED DEAD

FOREWORD

We can determine the young woman's final actions from the electronic signals sent to and from her cell phone. At 1:35 a.m., we know, her phone rang. Global Positioning Satellite data placed her location within an accuracy of a few feet to an apartment building on River Oaks Drive in North Myrtle Beach, S.C., where she lived with a roommate.

Up popped a local 843 number that matched no name in her list of contacts. Call records later obtained from the Frontier Communications linked that number to one of the nation's few operating pay phones, outside a Kangaroo Express gas station on the corner of Seaboard Street and 10th Avenue in Myrtle Beach.

The call lasted about four minutes and left her crying hysterically, a fact a jury would know only because a defense attorney would later fail to lodge a hearsay objection.

We know she called back the pay phone three times in rapid succession, never getting an answer, suggesting a frantic need to make a connection.

She then got into her car, a 2001 Dodge Intrepid registered to her father, and drove to a nearby restaurant called Longbeard's Bar & Grill on Carolina Forest Boulevard. She pulled into the corner of the dark parking lot. GPS put her near the Dumpsters. She called the pay phone back four more times, again getting no answer.

She next drove to the entrance of a housing development called Augusta Plantation down the street, then returned to

Longbeard's, and called the pay phone twice more—for a total of nine fruitless attempts at reaching somebody—before returning to her apartment. She may have stayed outside on the street. She may have gone inside.

It was now 3:16 a.m., a moonlit night, according to the National Weather Service.

She dialed another local 843 number. This one did come from a contact in her phone, one that she had once exchanged phone calls and text messages more than 1,000 times, but that she hadn't called in weeks.

Nobody answered. She dialed again at 3:17 a.m. and got a connection. The call lasted for 4:15 minutes. She then immediately started driving. GPS followed her down White River Road, to Forest Brook Road to Peachtree Road, a narrow, one-way road.

There she stopped.

She made more calls, got no answers. The last call was recorded at 3:41 a.m.

GPS data placed her final stop at Peachtree Landing, with nothing around her but the murky waters of the Waccamaw River and, beyond that, forest and wetlands, what a prosecutor later called "one of the darkest holes in Horry County."

We can only infer all this because of the limitations of modern technology. We know what phones called what numbers at what times from what locations.

To determine who actually spoke on those phones, we need witnesses, a confession, and additional physical evidence such as DNA, blood, hair, and fingerprints.

We didn't have that. All we would know was from that point on, nobody has seen or heard from Heather Elvis again.

1.

Around 4 a.m. on Wednesday, Dec. 18, 2013, Casey Guskiewicz pulled his Horry County Police Department cruiser down Peachtree Road to the boat launch. Guskiewicz was in the final stretch of his 5:45 p.m. to 6 a.m. graveyard shift, on routine patrol, driving solo through Sector 14 in the Central Precinct, "ensuring the safety and lives and property of Horry County," he'd later say in court.

A barrel-chested man with his brown hair in a military cut, Guskiewicz was in uniform: gray shirt with black epaulets, and shoulder patch bearing a hilltop farmhouse overlooking a stream and the beach with a cheery yellow sun.

His route took him down lonely country roads lined with telephone poles, mobile homes on grassy lots, mailboxes on posts, and dirt roads marked "private road." He passed the Sweethome Freewill Baptist Church with a pitched roof and brick walls, and neat white homes on big lots.

A turn at Peachtree Road plunged him into the Waccamaw National Wildlife Refuge. Houses stood on stilts due to periodic flooding of the Waccamaw River.

A stop sign emerged in the darkness. Without it, a person unfamiliar with the area would "drive straight into the water," he recalled. Just past the stop sign, the ramp descended into the Waccamaw River section of the Intracoastal Waterway. On either side of the landing were parking spots. To the east was a small trailer park with a half-dozen residences. To the west was "nothing but swamp," he said.

There he saw a dark-colored Dodge Intrepid sedan. It was parked—"awkwardly" was the word he used—in the middle of the boat landing facing the river. He shined his headlights on the car so he could make out the license plate. He ran the tags on his in-car computer and the Dodge came back clean, not stolen.

He walked up to the car and shined his flashlight through the driver's side rear window. The car was locked. He didn't see anybody in the front seat or the back. He didn't see any keys in the ignition or any sign of a cell phone on the seats. The seats and floorboards were littered with papers and what looked like food wrappers.

Guskiewicz scanned the landing. Not a soul. He shined his flashlight into the swamp on his right, shined it across the river. "No boats, no nothing," he said.

After five or six minutes, he left without calling it into the station, without filing a report, without notifying the registered owner. "It was just a vehicle parked at a boat landing," he said. Something he'd seen many times on his rounds.

Ominous at night, by day, the landing is known as a quiet, pleasant, picturesque spot in the county, a jumping off point for boating and fishing, where families would come for picnics and day trips on the Waterway. People left their cars there for days sometimes. Some parked them more considerately than others.

Shortly after 4 a.m., he left the landing to complete his rounds.

He may have missed Heather Elvis by less than a half-hour.

The Dodge Intrepid sat at the landing all through a cold and gray Dec. 18 and Dec. 19, when few, if any, boaters used the landing, until at 5 p.m. on the 19th, somebody reported it to police.

Kenneth Canterbury, a patrol officer in the south precinct of Horry County Police Department, which covers Socastee,

Myrtle Beach, Zuman, and Surfside, took the call of a suspicious vehicle.

Peachtree Landing didn't fall into his usual patrol route—he was in a different precinct—but he responded anyway. He drove down the same roads that Guskiewicz had taken that morning, arriving at the landing, he estimated, just after sunset, which the National Weather Service recorded as 5:10 p.m.

Burly and buzz-cutted, Canterbury could be Guskiewicz's brother. He saw the same dark Dodge Intrepid parked in the same haphazard fashion. Using his flashlight, he found the same lack of damage, the doors locked, the car empty, and the inside cluttered with paper. He, too, ran the tag. Not stolen, but registered to a name he recognized: Elvis.

Canterbury had grown up in Socastee and knew the Elvis family. Terry Elvis was a prominent local businessman who ran a sign shop with the whimsical name All Ways Stuck On You in the Market Common shopping center in Myrtle Beach. Terry's father had been Canterbury's barber. The officer had met Terry at least once, though didn't know him well.

The family had no known relations to the King of Rock and Roll. But there was an Elvis Presley sticker on the back of the Dodge.

Using the address on the car registration, Canterbury drove to Terry's house a few miles away in the town of Socastee. Terry answered the door.

The officer explained that he had found a car registered to Terry at the Peachtree Landing. Terry said that while the car was in his name, his daughter Heather drove it exclusively. Heather was 20 years old, lived in her own apartment in North Myrtle Beach and worked at a local restaurant as a hostess.

He had last seen her two days before, on Tuesday, Dec. 17, when she came by the house to pick up her mail. He hadn't spoken to her since. The family—Terry, wife Debbi,

Heather and her younger sister, Morgan, who still lived at home—had often gone to the landing when the kids were younger. He had no idea why the car would be parked there.

They both drove back to the landing in the patrol car. Together, they searched with flashlights around the car for a sign of Heather: a purse, clothing, shoes. They found nothing. Terry gave the officer his extra set of keys to the car. Wearing latex gloves, Canterbury opened the Dodge and poked around inside. It was hard to see what was there—the car was such a mess, which Terry said was not out of the ordinary for his daughter. The officer found Heather's driver's license. The photo showed a pretty young woman with light reddish hair, brown eyes and a warm smile.

He didn't find the woman's cell phone or purse.

It was now about 7 p.m. Terry called his daughter's cell phone. It went straight to voicemail. While it was not unusual to go days without seeing or speaking to her, Terry said she'd never done anything like this before. Heather had never left town without telling her father or mother. Terry dialed everybody he thought Heather could be with. Nobody knew.

Canterbury gave Terry a pair of latex gloves and let him drive the car back to his home. The officer then called his supervisor. The search for Heather Elvis had begun.

2.

Myrtle Beach has a dual identity. For much of the outside world, this is a Southern seaside playground with warm, humid days spent at clean, sandy beaches and exciting nights of dancing, karaoke and drinking at the restaurants and clubs. Tourism powers the local economy. Each year, more than 14 million visitors pour into a town with only 32,000 permanent residents—spring breakers, Canadian snowbirds, conventioneers, motorcycle club members, and golfers, lots of golfers.

Tiger Woods calls the area the "Mecca for golf." About 100 golf courses are located around Myrtle Beach, with 3.2 million rounds of golf played in 2017. One of the area's six institutions of higher learning is the Golf Academy of America, which offers a two-year associate of arts degree in golf operations and management.

Early June brings the Sun Fun Festival and the Coastal Uncorked food and wine festival, and Senior Week for recent high school graduates; March the Can-Am Days for the thousands of Ontario, Canada, visitors during their spring break; May the Harley Bike Week, a weeklong motorcycle rally, and Black Bike Week, the world's largest African American motorcycle rally.

Towering hotels and condos dominate the beachfront skyline. The Myrtle Beach SkyWheel, a giant Ferris wheel built in 2011, can be seen for miles and sparkles at night. In 2005, the $250 million entertainment development called

Broadway at the Beach opened, with 20 restaurants, 100 shops, three movie theaters, an aquarium, wax museum, and three hotels—all ringing a lagoon and spread across 350 acres carved into special zones with names such as New England Fishing Village and Celebrity Square.

When locals say they're going to "Broadway," they mean this complex. It was here that Heather Elvis worked at the Tilted Kilt hostess counter. This was a themed restaurant/bar in the tradition of the more famous Hooter's, the theme being kinky Scottish schoolgirl. The female employees wear plaid push-up bras, white halter tops tied just below the bust, midriff-exposing micro-kilts, white knee socks with bright red tassels, and high-heeled Mary Janes.

Heather represented the other side. There is a literal barrier between them and the resorts of Myrtle Beach: the Intracoastal Waterway, the great north-south barge canal of George Washington's dreams, made real starting in the 19th century, now running for 3,000 miles from Boston to the tip of Florida. Horry County's segment was the last, opened in 1936, by which time planes and railroads had long since made the transport of goods and people over canals obsolete.

When the Intracoastal Waterway was extended some 30 miles, with a 12-foot-deep, 90-foot wide trench, it was said to be the water's longest manmade ditch. It also cut Myrtle Beach off from the mainland, a problem solved by the construction of the Socastee Swing Bridge in 1936.

On Atlantic Ocean side of the Waterway are the hotels, restaurants and beaches; inland, the workers, the Horry County of humble houses, trailer parks and Walmart, of dense forests and long driveways with "No Trespassing" signs, of pickup trucks, which people call "vee-hickles," and guns—a bright red diamond-shaped county in a red state. In 2018, the state went 55 percent for Donald Trump, Horry County 67 percent.

People from the 1,200 square miles of Horry County pour the beers, cook the steaks and clean up after the people from outside world. It's a hospitality-based economy that's not always hospitable to the employees. They have to wrangle tips to supplement minimum wages and suffer without benefits. One trial witness would later say that Heather Elvis was listed as a part-time employee in the books, even though she pulled full-time hours.

While the resort draws outsiders, for the locals, Myrtle Beach's attractions hold limited appeal. One trial witness complained that here, in a fantasyland that promises on its website "fun days at the beach, lush natural wonders, and grand new adventures," there "isn't much to do" most of the time. Maybe drive to Broadway for karaoke; maybe go to the ballpark and watch the Pelicans, a minor league affiliate of the Chicago White Sox; maybe hang out with friends, drink and smoke pot.

The distinction between here and there runs deeply in Horry County. The county's official nickname is "Independent Republic." The words grace the patches worn by every police officer.

While that may seem to speak Southern pride—South Carolina was the first of 11 states to secede—the feeling of otherness predates the Civil War. Cut off from the rest of the state by swamps and rivers in the early days, Horry County's rugged citizenry had to make due on their own. The rest of South Carolina was seen as the "outside world." Even within the county, there are divisions. Myrtle Beach has the glitz; Socastee, where Heather grew up, on the other side of the swing bridge, the grit, with a whiff of resentment. "The community of Socastee predates the internationally famous coastal resort of Myrtle Beach by many years," the Socastee town website says. "The Socastee Bridge paved the way for the tremendous growth of the vacation metropolis."

Heather Elvis did not show up for her shift at the Tilted Kilt at Broadway at the Beach on Friday, Dec. 20, 2013. This, too, was out of character. Her manager described her to police as conscientious and hard working. She would call ahead if she were late and never failed to appear without notice.

As she was too young to work as a waitress and pour alcohol, Heather remained posted at the hostess desk, greeting customers, leading them to their tables, telling them that their server would be by shortly. Co-workers gushed about her bubbly personality, and her rapport with guests, many of them from somewhere else.

She liked her job, and posted about it often on social media. She liked the revealing uniforms. "My job over your job," she wrote on Facebook over a picture of herself and a coworker in the outfits. If anything, she seemed to revel in the shock value. On Twitter, she posted a close-up photo of cleavage in a Tilted Kilt bra with the caption, "We are a family friendly establishment."

If she had any shortcoming at work, it was her attachment to her cell phone. Despite a ban against having phones while on duty—almost a moot point as the uniforms offered no place to carry one—Heather would stash her phone under the hostess table and peek at it when she wasn't supposed to.

The fact that she didn't get in touch with her manager, hadn't used her phone since early Wednesday morning, and left behind her driver's license added up to foul play. Everyone said Heather would never just take off like this.

Police entered her name into the National Crime Information Database so that every law enforcement agency in the nation would know that she was missing. Another search of her car turned up her bank card and cosmetology license, recently obtained after taking classes. There were also receipts from places the afternoon before she disappeared: McDonald's and a Kangaroo Express gas station, both in Myrtle Beach. There was a pack of cigarettes, but no drugs or drug paraphernalia. There was no blood.

Police searched her apartment, built next to a golf course. Her apartment was out of the "Odd Couple," her roommate's room neat and clean, sweaters carefully folded on a shelf, items in the bathroom neatly stored, while Heather's room was a mess, the bed unmade, clothes strewn around.

Amid the clutter, police found her Tilted Kilt uniform in a bag. There were golf clubs, TV, computer and printer. On the nightstand were red plastic cups and a dirty plate. In the bathroom were a toothbrush, toothpaste, deodorant, and, propped on the edge of a sink, an empty pizza box. No sign of a struggle, no blood, no drugs.

It didn't look like she had planned to travel. There was a purple suitcase marked with a piece of tape that read "Heather." It was empty.

A call by police to local hospitals brought an early, false lead. Conway Medical reported a woman by her name was admitted at 3:04 p.m. the afternoon of Dec. 18 and released at 6:12 p.m. This, however, seemed to contradict two pieces of evidence found amid the rubble in her car—receipts from a Kangaroo Express in Myrtle Beach at 4:18 p.m., then a McDonald's 16 minutes later, when she presumably was still admitted.

The mystery was solved when the hospital called back to say they had made a mistake and that Heather Elvis had not been there; they had the wrong name.

By Friday night, a search operation was deployed that would grow to include seven local and state agencies. Boats from Horry County, Myrtle Beach, and the Department of Natural Resources searched the brown waters of the Intracoastal Waterway around Peachtree Landing. The state police, known by its acronym SLED for South Carolina Law Enforcement Division, sent up a helicopter to buzz the forests and shopping areas.

The Tilted Kilt's corporate offices donated digital advertising signs. A company called Lamar Advertising donated additional billboards. By nightfall Friday, 13 billboards lit up the Grand Strand stretch of beaches in the resort section with information about Heather's disappearance. Horry County police announced that detectives from the major crimes division were on the case and that a $10,000 reward was posted for "information leading to the closure of the case and the location of Heather Elvis."

Out of his sign shop, Heather's father, Terry, produced thousands of flyers and posters. "Please help us find our daughter," they read with a photo and the information about her brown/auburn hair and brown eyes and 5-foot-1, 118-pound frame. Beneath the phone, it said in capital letters:

"THIS IS OUR CHILD, OUR DAUGHTER, OUR REASON FOR LIVING. I BEG OF YOU, IF YOU HAVE ANY INFORMATION THAT MAY BE HELPFUL NO MATTER HOW SMALL, PLEASE CONTACT ME OR THE HORRY COUNTY POLICE DEPARTMENT AT THE FOLLOWING NUMBERS. YOUR IDENTITY WILL BE PROTECTED AND YOUR INFORMATION WILL BE APPRECIATED MORE THAN WE CAN EXPRESS WITH WORDS."

Terry Elvis then spoke to any media outlet that would listen, and most did, as he pleaded for anybody to share the smallest of information, "even if it was one lead they got, then it was worth it." Family friend Matt Stoddard also hit the airwaves, telling WFMB-TV that Heather's family was "really worried" and urged anyone who may have seen Heather since Tuesday to "get in touch with the family and call Horry County Police with any information that might be helpful because at this point, anything we can get will help try to find her."

The publicity generated what investigators thought was a hot lead. A young man named Evan German, who had met Heather when she and her roommate had attended a party at his beach house two months earlier, called police to say he thought he spotted her that Friday night.

Interviewed by investigators on Saturday, he said he was at a Myrtle Beach club called the Beaver Bar when he bumped into her. He said he told her, "Hey," and she said, "Hey," back, they hugged, and each went their separate ways.

At the request of police, the bar culled through surveillance footage and actually recorded the moment. German reviewed the tape. It wasn't Heather. The woman bore a slight resemblance to her, but she didn't have a dolphin tattoo on her arm as Heather did. Evan would later say the false sighting was an alcohol-fueled mistake. "I drank too much that night," he said.

On Sunday night, with Heather gone four days, friends and family gathered for a prayer at First Baptist Church of Myrtle Beach. The next day, the search resumed with law enforcement still focusing on the woods and waterways around Peachtree Landing.

The weather had been unusually cold, hovering around freezing at night, and with each passing hour, Heather's father grew more frantic. "I can't explain it. It's like having your heart torn out, 24 hours a day," he told WPDE-TV. "No sleep, you can't eat, just the worry, the worry is overwhelming. I'd give anything, anything to have her back safe."

State police conducted an electronic search, punching Heather's information into databases that tracked a wide variety of sources. She had not used a credit card or an ATM. She had not paid a utility bill, subscribed to a magazine, bought real estate or a car, filed an insurance claim or obtained a new driver's license. She hadn't been arrested, cited for speeding, or checked into a hospital. Her name didn't pop up in any morgues.

A "Find Heather Elvis" Facebook page went up, moderated by Stoddard and his wife, April, where people posted condolences, but no immediate leads of any value, while Terry Elvis continued to make the media rounds. He told WPDE through tears, "We miss her terribly. Her sister:

devastated. Her brother: devastated. Her mother and I: beyond devastated."

As the story began making national news, he told Fox News, "She's a good-hearted girl, always helpful and active in her church activities. Everybody loved her. To not hear from her for more than 24 hours is way out of character."

Christmas came with no trace of Heather, now missing for a week. Her family didn't celebrate and instead planned to leave up the frosted tree with white lights and keep the presents unopened until they found her.

By Dec. 28, civilians, who had been discouraged from joining the search so as to preserve any possible crime scenes, now were welcomed. The Cue Center for Missing Persons, a North Carolina-based non-profit that provides advocacy and logistical support in missing persons case, put out the word for volunteers with boats to assemble at the Peachtree Landing ramp that Saturday morning. More than 60 private sailors joined fire department boats going up and down the Waccamaw River from Myrtle Beach to Surfside Beach, eight miles down the coast.

Terry Elvis and the Tilted Kilt pumped another $10,000 into the reward fund, raising it to $20,000, and the "Find Heather Elvis" Facebook page beat the drum:

"IF YOU WERE AT OR NEAR PEACHTREE LANDING FROM 10pm TUESDAY, DECEMBER 17th UNTIL 6am WEDNESDAY, DECEMBER 18th, PLEASE CONTACT US!" a post said. "YOU MAY HAVE SEEN SOMETHING THAT YOU MAY OR MAY NOT HAVE REALIZED. YOUR HELP IS GREATLY APPRECIATED!"

Local businesses posted the missing poster and volunteers in reflective vests lined streets, handing out flyers. A company called Executive Helicopters put its craft in the air and the Olive Garden planned a fundraiser for the search effort.

It seemed that everybody in the Myrtle Beach community was worried about this young woman with a fresh-scrubbed, pretty face and radiant smile in her many social media posts now appearing in the news.

She was Horry County's own, born and bred. In a county of us and them, she was us. Everybody knew her, even if they'd never met her.

But they didn't know everything.

3.

The longer Heather Elvis remained missing, the younger and more innocent she became, until one day a prosecutor would call her a "young, little girl" and liken her, literally, to a Disney princess.

To her family, particularly her father, Terry, whose grief was palpable and very public, she was, of course, his beloved older daughter, snatched away just as a bright life spread out before her.

In the community, she was everybody's sister, everybody's daughter, every girl's BFF, so adorable with her bright smile, reddish hair and fair skin in those missing posters.

For the media, she was catnip, the prized great white missing female.

She had graduated two years earlier from St. James High School in Socastee, paying her dues in restaurant work while studying in her spare time to become a makeup artist.

"She's always had a job, even though I didn't require her to, she wanted to do it her way since she was 17," Terry Elvis told the true-crime blog, CrimeFeed.

He said just before she disappeared, she had landed a job at a local salon as a make-up artist, to begin work the week of Christmas. "The cosmetology thing came out of the blue, she wanted to be a make-up artist and work the runway. She was interested in being in Charlotte, Atlanta, and New York. The cosmetology thing was just a foot in the door, a local business."

Every photo seemed to show her clutching puppies and babies. Friends and family spoke of her love of children and ice cream, of drawing and painting and fashion design. Her father described her missionary trip three years earlier to Costa Rica, where she was captivated by the luminescent water, helped repair a house for a poor family and taught children to read.

"She has come to be everyone's sister, cousin, niece and child," family friend April Stoddard told *The State* newspaper. "She's at that age where you're going into adulthood and finding out who you are, where you're going and what you want to do. Your horizon is so open."

And now she was gone—stubbornly, cruelly gone.

Her father couldn't wrap his head around why her car would be found by the river. Heather and the family knew Peachtree Landing well, but, he said, "not at that hour of the night."

The Horry County Police Department gave regular updates on the various search operations, but otherwise revealed nothing of substance. The department spokesman, Lt. Robert Kegler, would only make vague assurances the investigation was "very active" and that "several people" were interviewed. But he wouldn't say whether police had a suspect, or even a person of interest, or if they had any idea what she was doing that night and what may have happened to her.

One of the unintended consequences of a case hitting the media is that certain facts emerge that run counter to the prevailing narrative.

The police term is victimology, the process of assessing the victim of the violent crime, examining their mannerisms and mental states, their circles of friends, their potential enemies. Often, this can be the fastest way to solving a crime.

The problem is that if some of that information gets out, it can open police to accusations that they're blaming the victim for the crime. It can also make the victim look very bad.

One of the first places police can now look is at a victim's social media pages. For Heather, the material was plentiful and potentially illuminating. She was, as her friends said, a relentless sender of tweets. They came in bursts, sometimes 10 or more in a day, and covered everything from a favorite song or swimsuit to something silly or clever she saw on somebody else's social media to whatever thought—the good, the bad and the profane—that happened to be pulsing through her mind at any given time, all expressed in that heightened OMG tone for which Twitter is known and loathed.

Her Twitter page under the "Moonchild" handle paints a portrait of a passionate young woman with a rebellious streak, still finding herself, loving good times, hot outfits, cold drinks, Katy Perry and friends who share the same and boyfriends who don't screw you over.

Suffice it to say the tweet, "I just wanna get stupid wasted, do fun shit like swim naked, go to wafflehouse play the music box thing & dance on the tables" is nothing they'd put on her missing posters.

Years from now, none of us will want to be remembered from our Twitter-selves. In truth, Heather's page looked like many other Twitter pages, one side of a multi-dimensional person, a young work in progress, what a prosecutor would astutely describe as a "20-year-old girl who was basically playing grownup."

And yet the fact that she was missing under very possibly violent circumstances demanded that even the most fleeting of messages be taken seriously, as when she tweeted on Jan. 26, 2013, "I'm moving to Australia soon," or on March 25, 2013, "I need to be in Florida like right now. I can't stand this distance."

The same held true when she hinted at romantic issues, as in this tweet from just two days later, "And for some reason

I wish I was the one you were making happy, not her. I hate her."

For deeper insights, police went to Heather's roommate, Brianna Warrelmann. Both women had worked together at the Tilted Kilt and partied together in Myrtle Beach. As the apartment showed, Brianna was the cleaner one. She also was protective of Heather, treating her like a little sister.

"She was the rebellious child," Brianna said later in court, repeating what she told police. "She had her own views on what she thought her life should be and obviously for her parents it wasn't the same." Brianna saw it as nothing more than Heather trying to find her way in life. "I know I put my parents through hell and back, and so did she," she said. "I don't think that her and her parents saw eye to eye about certain choices that she made in her life."

Heather's coworker, Megan Bonfert, a server at Tilted Kilt, said, "Heather felt like the outcast in her family," calling herself a "rebel without a cause." Megan chalked it up to her being "a typical teenage girl," even if Heather were now 20.

Not long after graduating from high school, Heather fell into a bad place. She dated a young man who was "emotionally and verbally abusive," Brianna said later. "He was controlling." Others said the abuse had turned physical. One of Heather's friends, Sydney Lee Moffitt, said that in the summer of 2012, Heather appeared with bruise on her neck. Living with her parents at the time, Heather "didn't want to go home," Sydney later said in court. She didn't want anybody to know. She tried to hide it, wearing a scarf during the sweltering South Carolina summer.

Sydney, who was pregnant, gave Heather a place to stay. Heather spent two to three months on the couch in the apartment Sydney shared with her boyfriend. Sydney never got a full story from Heather, but clearly the boyfriend was to blame. Sydney had one rule. "I just told her she could stay with me as long as he couldn't be around my apartment," said Sydney.

Going into 2013, Heather would again find herself temporarily homeless. She was "kicked out of the house on numerous occasions," Brianna said. For an unknown amount of time, Heather lived out of her car. She also crashed at the home of her Tilted Kilt boss, manager Jessica Cooke, who didn't ask questions. "I know that she had an argument at home and wasn't there, that's all I know," she later said.

At some point, Heather and the ex came to an understanding. She forgave him. She moved into his apartment, now as platonic friends, until he wanted to rekindle a relationship with another ex-girlfriend. When that woman arrived, Heather got the boot. This was around Thanksgiving of 2013. She needed another place to stay. Brianna had an extra room in her apartment. They became roomies.

Heather had troubles, but she wasn't alone. She found comfort and support in a circle of coworkers and friends, male and female, and by December of 2013, she was ready to date again.

On the evening of Tuesday, Dec. 17, 2013, a young man appeared at her apartment door. It was their first date. It would also be their last.

4.

Stephen Schiraldi was a sauté chef for the lunch rush at the upscale seafood restaurant Wicked Tuna in Murrells Inlet, a former fishing village turned popular tourist destination south of Myrtle Beach. Twenty-one years old, Stephen was skinny with a boyish face and dark hair. He wore glasses in square frames. He lived in Myrtle Beach with his younger brother and mother, who worked the night shift at Walmart.

Stephen knew Heather from St. James High School. A year ahead of her, Stephen did not run in her social circle; his knowledge of her came from "just seeing her around." A junior, she had darker, auburn hair, was petite and vivacious with big brown eyes.

In recent weeks, they started following each other on Instagram and "just got to talking and commenting on one of her pictures," he later said. Finally, he asked her out online, and she accepted.

It was Brianna who had tipped police to Stephen. He immediately became a major person of interest in Heather's disappearance. On the afternoon of Dec. 20, investigators arrived at Wicked Tuna. They went to what Stephen called "a private place" and had a talk. He asked for no lawyer. He said he had nothing to hide. He hadn't known Heather for long, but his concern for her, he said, was genuine.

According to an account later given in court, Stephen told investigators he picked up Heather at her apartment near the River Oaks Course down the street from the Midas muffler shop at 7 p.m. She was even more beautiful than in high school. She had gained a little weight, a source of complaints to friends.

She got in his 1998 blue-gray Ford Ranger pickup and they went to a beachfront Mexican restaurant called Banditos Cantina in the heart of the Myrtle Beach resort area, a couple blocks north of the SkyWheel.

They had dinner, but no drinks, he said. Afterward, they took a drive around Horry County for 90 minutes, which they spent talking. Heather happened to mention that she'd never learned how to drive a car with a stick shift. Friends had tried to teach her, but she never got the hang of it.

They headed south to the Inlet Square Mile, where in the empty parking lot, Stephen gave her a lesson in his manual-transmission pickup. In 20 minutes, she was doing "pretty well," he recalled: no grinding of gears, no major damage. She was so excited, she had him snap of a picture of her at the wheel, which she sent to her father to prove that she'd finally mastered the stick shift.

The photo arrived on her father's phone at 10:43 p.m. with the message: "Just learned to drive stick. I'm a pro."

She has her left hand on the steering wheel, her right gripping the console gearshift. In her lap is her cell phone in a sparkly red case. She's smiling from ear to ear.

After the lesson, they drove 10 minutes to Stephen's house, where they watched a movie in his bedroom. "After the movie, it was kind of late so I took her home," he later recalled in court. He estimated to police that he dropped her off at her apartment between 2 a.m. and 2:30 a.m. on what was now Wednesday, Dec. 18.

Spending only five minutes at her apartment, they made plans to meet again the next day after his work shift ended at 3 p.m. He drove home. They later exchanged text messages and an approximately five-minute phone call before he fell asleep.

Stephen insisted that all evening, Heather seemed "happy" and "friendly." He had no reason to think they wouldn't see each other again. And he didn't worry when she didn't return his calls and Facebook messages the next day. "Maybe her phone was dead or she lost her phone, left it somewhere," he'd recall. "I just assumed that she was busy and she would get back to me."

Stephen denied having anything to do with her disappearance.

None of this made the news at the time, police keeping the investigation under tight wraps. (In his many interviews in the weeks after his daughter's disappearance, Terry Elvis never mentioned the photo or Stephen to help preserve the integrity of the investigation; Terry even spoke to Stephen the night the officer arrived. It's not known what they said.)

By all accounts, police believed him. The interview lasted less than 20 minutes. He wasn't arrested and never gave a further formal statement.

Investigators didn't think they needed one.

5.

The first bones were found on New Year's Eve day. A search party looking for Heather Elvis came across them in heavy woods in North Myrtle Beach, about 25 miles from Peachtree Landing. Horry County police spokesman Lt. Peter Cestare described them as "adult skeletal remains." It couldn't be immediately determined if they were male or female.

For days, searches trudged through wild country, forested wetlands with moss-covered deciduous trees such as cypress, tupelo, red maple, elm, oaks, and gums that shelter wading birds such as ibis and egrets, swallow-tailed kite, osprey, wood stork, vixen red fox, deer, wild turkey, and black bear. Strands of tall, slender, century-old, long-leaf pines stand where the endangered red-cockaded woodpeckers nest.

The remains would have been easy to miss. They were scattered, probably by animals.

That day, the search continued—volunteers and professionals scouring the woods and waterways of Horry County. Every operation began with promise and ended with disappointment. Then on Dec. 31, 2013, searchers made the grisly discovery in a thick forest in North Myrtle Beach, about 25 miles away from Heather Elvis' car was found.

That night, Heather's father posted a grim message on Facebook, a poem that spoke directly to her, beginning:
Surrounded by darkness
I am afraid
Of what I do not know

The poem spoke of holding his arms open for "you to come back," yet she was nowhere to be found, except in his mind when he closed his eyes. He ended by beseeching Heather to help him find her:

"God please I can no longer do this."

At any given time, as many as 90,000 people are missing in the United States, just half of them female, more than half white. The Heather Elvis case was one of the few to dominate the news, a result, no doubt, of her good looks, gender, and race, along with the mystery surrounding the case and her family's frank and public expressions of grief.

But there were others. Including Jamie Lynn Cross.

On Dec. 22, 2013, just four days after Heather disappeared, 24-year-old Jamie left her home near Myrtle Beach, saying she was going to dinner with a man from Conway. She was last seen getting into the back seat of a Volvo station wagon that drove away. Days passed without a word from her.

The missing posters said she stood a half-inch shy of 6 feet and weighed 240 pounds. She was wearing a bright pink shirt that matched her cascading neon pink hair. In case she had reverted to an earlier look, other posters featured a more subdued version of Jamie with dark brown hair pulled back, cat-eye glasses and a demure black dress with polka dots.

That a woman four years older than Heather Elvis disappeared just four days after she did could not be ignored. Police and activists started scouring the case files for similar missing persons case and came up with another one, nearly forgotten but bearing some similarities.

In April of 2009, 17-year-old Brittanee Drexel, like Heather a pretty blonde with a rebellious streak, snuck out of her house in Rochester, N.Y., and went down to South Carolina for spring break without her mother's permission. A security camera at the trendy Bluewater Resort on Ocean Boulevard captured the high school junior leaving the hotel on April 25 at about 9 p.m.

She left with a group of male friends and was seen walking along Ocean Boulevard toward the Bar Harbor Hotel, where she was staying with other girls, texting her boyfriend along the way. She never arrived, and security cameras caught no sight of her. Police at the time suspected she was kidnapped and most likely dead.

Myrtle Beach Police Capt. David Knipes told ABCNews.com at the time that "nobody's been cleared." Her boyfriend, John Grieco, then 19, who wasn't with her on the trip, said, "I think there was foul play. I do not believe at all that she is a runaway ... or that she committed suicide."

Then there was Zack Malinowski.

That previous August, after a game of basketball, Zack, a tall, skinny 19-year-old from the town of Aynor, 30 miles northwest of Myrtle Beach, dropped a friend off in Conway, then returned to Aynor with another friend. The pair went to a woman's house. At 11:30 p.m., Zack left, saying he wanted to get something to eat.

Eight days later, his dark purple Chevrolet Beretta was found in the woods of Aynor. It was destroyed by fire. Zack was never heard from again. Two men were arrested for investigation of kidnapping and murdering Zack, but charges were dropped as police pursued other charges against them. No more action was taken in Zack's case. Zack's body had not been found.

Young people were disappearing in Horry County and nobody could find them. The cases illustrated that behind the boosterism—"Happiness comes in waves" is Myrtle Beach's tourism slogan—the county can be a dangerous place, particularly for women, with law enforcement and prosecutorial resources stretched thin.

Waccamaw Publishers, the family-run media company that operates the *Carolina Forest Chronicle* and other community newspapers and the local news website MyHorryNews.com, provided brave, serious coverage of the Heather Elvis case, fighting to obtain sealed records, scoring one scoop after another, and never shying away from butting heads with the local officials. "Horry County murder cases stack up," read the headline over a story nobody in a county dependent on tourist dollars would want to see.

Horry County's prosecutors office, which is called the Solicitor's Office, had just 15 attorneys handling an average of 560 cases each. The American Bar Association recommends a load of 150 cases. The office managed to set an all-time record for resolving murder cases, but still had 50 murder cases pending. Officials blamed gangs, drugs, and shootings.

South Carolina, over all, had the sixth highest violent crime rate in the nation, and was second in the U.S. for the number of women killed by men. Overall, South Carolina had 558 violent crimes for every 100,000 people, well above the national average of 386 for each 100,000 residents.

So when volunteers found the human bones on New Year's Eve day in North Myrtle Beach, it sent shockwaves through the region.

The next day, more bones were found.

The Elvis family endured tense moments and grappled with mixed emotions. If it weren't Heather, then it could be somebody else. Another missing person. Another anxious family, bracing themselves for the worst.

An initial inspection showed the remains could not have been Heather's. They had been lying there for too long, maybe three years.

They weren't Jamie Cross's, either. She quickly surfaced, alive and well. Police spoke to her by phone, then met her in person to verify her identity. She was in good health and surprised to find that people were looking for her. Police concluded that as an adult, she had every right to drop off the map when she wanted. No charges were filed.

The bones also couldn't have been Brittanee's. Additional analysis showed the bones were those of a male. Her mother, Dawn Drexel, issued a statement similar to those issued for weeks by Heather's father, one of hope mixed with caution mixed with heartache.

"There are many missing children and adults in the region who have families suffering in anticipation of this latest news and who alongside of our family await for a resolution as well," she said. "I ask at this time to please wait for investigators to make a positive identification and be allowed to do their job. We need to respect the process along with the realization this could be any of our missing loved ones. I encourage all media to revisit the case files and feature our missing. It is so vital to keep these cases out in the public."

That left Zack. DNA testing could take months. The community could do nothing more for now than pray and continue searching. A shout-out for volunteers was posted on the Find Heather Elvis page to turn out the following Friday, Saturday and Sunday. With the weather turning cold and sour, they were told to "dress appropriately" in pants, outdoor boots and rain gear.

On Friday morning, some 100 people turned out with temperatures in the low 20s at the assembly site at a tent outside the River City Cafe near the Socastee Swing Bridge across the Waccamaw River. Volunteers solicited tips, even anonymous ones. "What might be insignificant to you, might be the piece of the puzzle we're missing," said Bill Barrett, identified by WPDE as a concerned parent and volunteer. The searchers then fortified themselves with coffee, got split into teams of 15 each, and fanned out into the dark forests.

Among the volunteers was Zack Malinowski's stepfather, Lonnie Jordan, who told WMBF-TV, "The actual peace of mind you get for seeing boots on the ground, going through the woods, going through the water. The lengths they go through ... this is the peace of mind you can receive."

A post went up on the Find Heather Elvis page: "This is how a community becomes a close knit area. Terry and the

Elvis Family have many friends helping. Thanks to you all of you from the bottom of my heart."

But Terry Elvis's patience was wearing thin. With Heather now missing for three weeks, the Elvis family began to express frustration with police. "At night, I feel like they are at square zero. I don't know where they are at, to be honest with you," Terry told Fox News. "I know they're working diligently. I know they're following every lead that they get."

With no news on the investigative front, all Terry could do was speak out. The next day, Jan. 7, the dean of TV true crime, Nancy Grace, went live to Myrtle Beach for a segment about what she called the "desperate search" for the "hostess at a local restaurant."

"Guys," Grace told her audience, "this girl is just 20 years old. She is a student. She's working, also studying. With me tonight, making a plea for your help, her parents are with us live, Debbi and Terry Elvis, joining us from Myrtle Beach."

Terry updated Grace on the last communication he had with his daughter: The photo she texted him of her learning the stick shift. Grace then pressed the couple on whatever they may know about the police investigation, starting with whether they knew if police had any surveillance camera footage from Heather's apartment.

"I'm not sure if there was at her apartment," said Heather's mother. "I know the police department, Horry County police and all the different agencies that are working with them, have looked for every surveillance video that she might have been in prior to her going missing, and then again after. And they've got help going through the hours and hours of surveillance video that they've collected."

Another guest, Michael Smith, editor of the *Carolina Forest Chronicle*, jumped in to say that the local media didn't know much, either, noting that the only thing they had to go on was a police report that had been heavily redacted.

"The date drops her off after dinner. And that's confirmed. She goes in. She calls friends to tell them about her date. That's in the wee morning hours, she's calling on the phone and texting."

"But then what happens there, Michael? What happens, Michael Smith?" Grace asked. "What's the next known thing, her car turns up?"

"Right. Pretty much. It's difficult to say," he said. "There are elements of the official police report that are still redacted, so it's difficult to say what else police know, other than that."

Back to the parents, Grace asked if police had confided where their daughter's cell phone was last used. Terry said all he knew was that the phone was last used at 3:41 a.m., based on information from their shared phone plan.

"Terry, was that pinged back to her apartment?" asked Grace.

"At this time, they won't really confirm where it was pinged to," he said.

"Did they find her purse and her cell phone at the apartment?"

"Her purse and her cell phone are missing along with her," Terry said. "Everything else looks to be where it's supposed to be."

Grace then addressed her audience. "Everyone, there is a $25,000 reward to help find Heather. She's just a 20-year-old girl. Her parents are begging for your help tonight," she said. "Please help us find Heather."

Two days later, "Good Morning America" did a segment about the woman "who seems to have simply vanished." Terry Elvis was back on the airwaves. "No amount of attention, no amount of law enforcement, no amount of work, effort that I do or anybody does is ever going to be enough until she is back home again."

Showing scenes of the family's Christmas tree still up, Heather's sister urged everybody to "take a moment to hold their family and tell them they love them," while her mother said the family was "just waiting for the right person to come forward and say: I saw something, or I heard something or I know something or I did something."

By week's end, another search party went out, this one from Peachtree Landing, hoping to cover about 300 acres. All they found were animal bones and garbage, including a sofa and a barbecue grill.

Another fundraiser to keep funding the searches and reward was held, this one selling double chocolate caramel nut clusters, and the Elvis family reached out to Gov. Nikki Haley for help. "If there is anything you can do in the search for Heather, I ask that you do whatever you can to help," the post states on the Find Heather Elvis Facebook page. "Your personal contact is requested on this matter. Please respond quickly."

When Haley swung through Myrtle Beach three days later, on Jan. 17, to give a speech to the Chicora Rotary to laud her accomplishments after three years in office, she announced she had taken the rare step for a governor of personally interceding in the search for Heather Elvis. She said she had been in contact with the family and state and local police to offer her "thoughts and prayers" and to pledged to do "everything we can" to find Heather, including "additional support" if needed.

"We try and avoid direct contact because there are so many missing people in South Carolina," Haley said. "This family, in particular, raised quite a few concerns and needed some extra attention, and so we did finally get to talk to them and make sure that their concerns were put to rest. We did everything we can to help them so they feel confident through this process."

The police department trotted out Lt. Kegler. When pressed on what police knew about Heather's movements the night she disappeared, he said, "There is no clear indication of why she left the apartment." He continued to say a task force "continues to receive and follow up on leads or tips," and that they were working with the Elvis family.

What he didn't say was that police had a lead, one that would break the case wide open -- and tear the community apart.

6.

"I was actually there when this all started."

Brianna Warrelmann said it was a summer night in July of 2013. Brianna, Heather and other workers from the Tilted Kilt got free passes to a Pelicans baseball game. Afterward, Heather gave Brianna ride back to the restaurant where she'd parked her car. "We went back to Tilted Kilt and we set on the back deck and had fries," she recalled.

That's when the restaurant's handsome, brown-haired, blue-eyed maintenance man walked by.

He had been building a cart to carry the umbrellas to the front of the restaurant. Heather's face brightened. Brianna quoted Heather as saying, "Look at him. I want to jump his bones."

He came by, sat down at their table and started talking to her. "They stayed actually past closing time at the restaurant," Brianna recalled. "I ended up leaving early that night and watched them talk outside in the parking lot of the Tilted Kilt by his truck."

On July 7, 2013, Heather tweeted: "The guy who builds things at my job makes me cream myself #wetdreams."

A second tweet that same day in all capital letters underscored those sentiments: "ONE OF THESE DAYS I WILL DRAG THAT MAN INTO THE MOP CLOSET AND HAVE MY WAY WITH HIM LORD HAVE MERCY."

Sidney Moorer was 37 years old, nearly twice Heather's age. Friendly and low-key, he worked when the restaurant was closed, cleaning it up for when it opened the following the morning. He would wait for Heather to come to work and bring her bagels and coffee. "It was definitely more than friendship. You could tell that both of them cared about each other," Brianna said. "If she needed money, he brought her that. He brought her Starbucks because she was obsessed with Starbucks."

Jessica Cooke, the front of the house manager at Tilted Kilt, said Sidney had been there for about six months. "When he started working there, he met everybody. He was friendly with everybody," she recalled. "Heather seemed to have a fondness for him. They started hanging out at the hostess stand and talking and having conversations."

One of Heather's bad habits was peeking at her phone at the hostess stand when she should have been alert to new customers. "They're not allowed to have their phones, but she always had it. She would get in trouble for having her phone at the hostess stand," Cooke recalled. One day, Heather needed to charge her phone. Cooke told her to do in the upstairs office, citing the no-phones-on-the-restaurant-floor rule.

"The office is always locked. I was up there doing computer work and her phone was continually going off," Cooke recalled. "So I looked at it to see who it was, and it was Sidney Moorer who texted her, saying what she is doing." Cooke scrolled through the messages and "one in particular that set a red flag in my head was that they were talking about how they had sex on the back patio of Tilted Kilt."

Using the phone at the hostess stand was one thing. Having sex with the janitor on the patio was another, and before long, everybody at the restaurant knew about it. Brianna also knew and urged Heather to break it off. Some of the servers weren't happy. They began harassing her, giving her the cold shoulder, making nasty remarks behind her back.

Finally, somebody left an anonymous message on the office blackboard: "Hey, ladies, please stop fucking the maintenance man. He's married."

Not just married, but with children. Sidney grew up in Summerville, S.C., 100 miles to the southwest of Myrtle Beach, a quaint Southern hamlet with old plantations dating back to the 1600s amid a wetlands forest with moss drooping from trees. Like Myrtle Beach, Summerville relies on tourist dollars, but sells itself as an "idyllic, small Southern town" with hundreds of historically listed buildings, more akin to Charleston, 20 miles away, than the gaudier playpen of Myrtle Beach.

According to the *Berkeley Observer*, Sidney attended Lord Berkeley Academy, now called St. John's Christian Academy, in the nearby town of Moncks Corner. He was one of two boys. His parents remained in Berkeley County.

Sometime in the late 1990s, Sidney packed up for Myrtle Beach, like many others looking for work in what was then a rapidly growing resort, where every week it seemed a new hotel or theme restaurant opened. The Hard Rock was the first restaurant in the new Broadway at the Beach development, its pyramid-shaped building a longtime fixture on the shores of the development's 23 acres across the water from where the Tilted Kilt would be.

Sidney would go on to leverage his restaurant experience by opening his own cleaning and maintenance company, hired by the biggest restaurants in the county, including Olive Garden, Red Lobster, Sticky Fingers Ribhouse, Longbeard's Bar & Grill and Tilted Kilt.

It was at the Hard Rock where Sidney met a waitress with big blond hair, a big personality, and a passion for rock 'n' roll. Tammy Caison heralded from Socastee from a family that dated its history in Horry County for generations. Her father was a welder, her mother a gospel singer and server. She had a younger sister named Ashley.

At Socastee High School, Tammy was involved with Students Against Drunk Driving, the Art Club, and the school newspaper, graduating in 1990. "I actually got a scholarship for journalism and I turned it down, crazily turned it down," she later said in court, "because I wanted to stay and watch my only sister grow up. She was only 5 years old. And after that, I just started waiting tables and bartending as I got old enough to bartend."

A classmate recalled Tammy as a rock music fan who had her picture taken with the lead singer of the '80s hair band Warrant. A relative told WMBF-TV that Tammy was more than just a fan.

"When she was in her teens, she was, I call them groupies, followed rock bands around," said the relative, who wished to remain anonymous. "[She was] bragging about being with them and stuff like that."

Years later, Tammy told friends about her colorful past on an online chat page. "In the late 80s I was big into the whole rock n roll scene. Long haired pretty boys, bubble gum metal (Metallica & Punk too but definitely not junk like Iron Maiden or Death Metal ew!)," she wrote.

On Facebook, she wrote, "My parents were always liberal with me and let me do about anything I wanted and although I've partied with some of the biggest names bands/celebs on this Planet not once have I tried drugs! (Not even pot when I was in a room full of people snorting coke and shooting heroin into their arms.) I've seen and been around things that would make you cringe, yet not participated in the acts. Why? Because I was raised to know better."

She adored her parents and as an adult, would live on their property. But her heart always belonged to music. "I never wanted to be a rock star myself, but I wanted to marry one. I could have married one, or at least moved to New Orleans with him and be his woman for the rest of my life. Anyway, I took a different route in the mid '90s and for the better," she said. She found out that there were different ways to remain in the rock world and stay true to her self. "I wanted to be BFFs with all of these people and the only way to do it without being a slimy piece of, well you guys know I mean, was to work in the business."

That's when she developed her love of photography. She would claim to have photographed dozens of rock stars, starting with the band Warrant. "They were pretty hot at the time (not in looks but on MTV)," she said. "That was my first paying job and I never looked back."

She would refer to the members of the band as "some of my closest friends in 1989 and the early '90s. "Good thing too because they toured with some rockin' bands and I used it to my advantage," she wrote. "Over the years I've met, gotten to know, hung out with, worked with, played with … more than 100 signed bands."

By the mid-'90s, she had traded in this lifestyle for something closer to home, working at the new Hard Rock Cafe in Myrtle Beach. She waited tables at the Hard Rock from about 1995 through 1998, a job she would describe with passion. "I made a killing too! Especially during the summer!" she wrote. "I would claim $50,000 a year! … We're talking 10-15 years ago and a menu that was typically 50 percent less! I know a lot of servers still making a killing there."

When she met Sidney there, he had bit of a rock edge. Photos showed him with longer hair and usually a goatee. They dated less than a year before getting married at Ocean View Baptist Church, and honeymooned on a Royal Caribbean Cruise, followed by a trip to Walt Disney World in Florida.

Disney would replace rock 'n' roll as Tammy's obsession (many of the details of her personal life come from a chat room for Disney fanatics called Disboards). She adored the fact that Sidney seemed to have an untapped love of Disney that his mother never recognized.

On the Disney chat board, she wrote, "He grew up five hours from WDW"—Walt Disney World—"and not one time did his family take him there as a child. ... How can someone not take their kids to Disney? Especially back when tickets were less than $20! Hello.".

The first time Sidney went to Walt Disney World was on their honeymoon. She said he took one look at the castle and it was "love at first sight for Sidney. He had been a fan of the cartoons & Walt since he was a baby, but after this first visit to the Magic Kingdom he was hooked," she wrote, adding, "It has only gotten worse over the past 15 years, not that this is a bad thing."

He was so immersed in Disney-ana that she posted a photo of him posed as a Pirate of the Caribbean with a pea coat with big cuffs and buttons, a sash and wide belt (offset by a backwards baseball cap). The photo was taken on the cruise ship The Dream in 2007 on "Pirate Night," she wrote, "before he grew his hair out. He knows how much I love long hair on men, so once again he's letting it grow."

A year after their marriage, their first son was born, followed by a daughter in 2001 and another son in 2005. They moved into her parents' property. Tammy home-schooled the children while operating her own travel agency, Magical Vacations, specializing in Disney parks.

Along the way, Sidney appeared to have flirted with show business. Reporters dug up his page on Exploretalent. com, which calls itself the Internet's largest audition site for actors, models, musicians, dancers and production crew. It didn't go far. He entered no résumé information or details about himself, but did include several photos. There was no mention of him ever getting acting or modeling jobs.

Instead, he started Palmetto Maintenance LLC. Restaurant managers would tell reporters that he was a diligent worker and came highly recommended. Even after his world crumbled, and nobody it seemed would so much as talk to him, he could still land jobs.

Heather's relationship with the married maintenance man had been going on for about three months when she got a call. The woman identified herself as Sidney's wife and said that she knew all about the affair. Heather's boss, Cooke, recalled, "Heather freaked out. She wanted to leave. She said, 'I'm sorry, I'm very nervous.'" The usually sunny Heather suddenly became "jittery" and "extremely nervous," said Cooke.

Only it wasn't Sidney's wife. It was two of the servers making a prank call. "She was getting a lot of conflict with other girls, that she was getting what she deserved by sleeping with a married man," said her coworker, Megan.

Although the prank was revealed, Heather and Sidney broke up in October of 2013. Accounts would conflict about who ended it. But all agreed Heather was crushed. "Heather was very sad. She wasn't her normal self," Cooke recalled. "She was kind of upset that the relationship was no longer because she actually had feelings. It seemed to me that she really had true feelings for him."

Heather was still trying to get back on her feet when a text message arrived. This one wasn't a prank. It came from Sidney's phone number.

It was a photo of Sidney Moorer. It appeared his wife had taken the picture. Sidney was staring straight into the camera, smiling. He was giving his wife oral sex.

7.

Police said nothing officially to the media about Heather's affair with Sidney Moorer. Nor did her friends, coworkers and family, who all knew about it. But Heather's summer relationship had become the worst-kept secret in Horry County.

The Moorer family felt the stares at the grocery store, heard the snide remarks uttered under the breath. Then they were bombarded by Twitter and Facebook comments—nasty, accusatory comments. People began to lurk around their property, some of them openly carrying guns. The Moorers said they would complain to police, but that the local authorities ignored their pleas.

Finally, on Jan. 17, one month after Heather disappeared, Tammy Moorer apparently couldn't take it anymore. Her Facebook page, normally an outpouring of love for Sidney, her children and anything Disney, took a savage turn.

"Well Sidney cheated on me in the months of Sept/Oct with a psycho whore who has since went missing," it said.

Then the Waccamaw Publishers dropped a bombshell, publishing the full contents of the heavily redacted police report. The report said Heather's roommate, Brianna Warrelmann, had told police that she had gotten a call from Heather the night she disappeared and that Heather "seemed like she was crying and upset."

According to Brianna, Heather was so emotional because she had just spoken on the phone with a married man whom

Heather knew. The man, who was twice Heather's age, told Heather he had left his wife and wanted to be with her, according to the newspaper report.

According to police documents cited by the newspaper, officers tracked down the man and he admitted to speaking with Heather that night, but insisted they hadn't seen each other since October and that he had "called her to tell her to quit calling him and that was it."

What's more, Terry Elvis also knew the man's identity. According to the newspaper, the night Heather disappeared, Terry contacted T-Mobile and found several calls back-and-forth between his daughter and this older man until the early morning hours of Dec. 18.

Because the man had not been arrested or charged, Waccamaw Publishers declined to identify him.

But many people knew the newspaper was talking about Sidney Moorer.

At first, Terry Elvis didn't comment. Instead, he penned a Jan. 21 essay for the millennial website XO Jane. "I am living a nightmare," he wrote, adding that wouldn't force him to give up hope. "The desire to find Heather and bring her home safe consumed my life now, there was no stopping. The word 'quit' did not exist for me on this task. We will find my daughter. We will find Heather Elvis."

That same day, he was back on HLN, this time talking to Jane Velez-Mitchell. HLN had found Heather's more provocative Twitter posts, including the one about how she was "in way too deep, but watch me get deeper."

Velez-Mitchell put the question directly to Terry: "According to some reports, sir, Heather was in contact with this older man, up until 6 a.m. on the day of her disappearance. Without naming names, because this person has not been named as a suspect, what do you know about this 37-year-old man, sir?"

"Well, I know that, according to police reports, and the phone records, she had been in contact with this person,"

Terry said, appearing uncomfortable. "I'm not sure of the length of time that they had known each other."

"Where did she meet him, and has he been in contact with authorities? Is—is his whereabouts known?"

"His whereabouts is known. And they have—the authorities have been in contact with him. I don't know the extent. But I know that they did meet at one of Heather's jobs."

The police report had also mentioned a second man, one who may have worked at the Tilted Kilt and had been abusive toward Heather.

"Had your daughter ever talked to you about man troubles, about—she's a beautiful, young woman working at this place where she's—you know, some have compared it to sort of like a Hooter's restaurant. Because, obviously, they hire attractive young women who dress in a sexy fashion. There's nothing wrong with that. I'm not in any way passing judgment. I'm just saying that that can create a situation where men come in, they get fixated on her. Or did she mention anything about either of these men to you ever?"

"She had never mentioned anything about being harassed or anything," he said. "I was given quite a bit of information from her about the job. She would tell us that, after her shift was over, one of the managers would always walk the girls to their car."

This marked the first time the national media had linked the sexy-themed Tilted Kilt and Heather's case. "It wasn't my first choice of job for her, of course," he said. "She's my daughter, but she's 20 years old, and she makes her own decisions. There was never any mention of any type of harassment, or any customer problems."

The case was now dividing the people of Horry County into one of two camps. You were either for the Elvis family or the Moorer family. Social media had violent overtones. One Facebook post threatened, "The police are watching, but its [sic] time to start doing your job and make someone talk," the post reads. "If the police dont [sic] do it first the citizens will."

The Moorers filed four harassment complaints with police, saying they feared for their safety. Police traced at least one inflammatory Facebook post to a local Myrtle Beach man. Garrett Ryan Starnes, 25, was arrested and charged with obstruction of justice. Police said that post and at least one other "created a community reaction that diverted investigating officers."

Then police got wind that another man was conducting his own investigation, talking to at least one of the witnesses already interviewed by police, in what appeared to be an attempt to find out covertly what detectives were doing.

Police identified that man as an Elvis family friend, William Christopher Barrett, 52, the same Bill Barrett quoted in the local news helping with the searches. Barrett was arrested for investigation of obstruction of justice. Barrett also was accused of searching a location and finding "potential evidence," but not telling police.

Lt. Kegler said, "There is a difference between providing law enforcement with tips and misleading law enforcement with false information."

Both men were booked at J. Reuben Long Detention Center before being released on $2,500 bond.

The Moorers would file three more police reports. In one, Terry Elvis is referred to as a "suspect." A witness was quoted as saying Terry drove by the Moorers' house multiple times, photographed the Moorers' house and made threats. (Terry was never arrested or charged).

Another report alleged someone took a shot at his family—not once, but twice. Reached by WMBF, Terry declined to comment.

It wasn't all directed at the Moorers. On Feb. 4, shortly after 1 p.m., two men in a Jeep drove up to Terry Elvis at The

Market Common and one yelled, "We already have Heather. Morgan is next," referring to Heather's younger sister.

The Jeep then sped off. Terry didn't recognize the men and police put out a public plea for help. The vehicle was described as a mid-2000 model Jeep Wrangler, dark black in color (not shiny), with blacked-out rims, lifted with a black ragtop, a tubular rear bumper and no license plate. Neither the men nor their Jeep were ever found.

Two days later, Sidney filed a police report alleging that while he was driving with his wife and children, a light-colored Ford truck sped up behind them and somebody fired two shots from an automatic weapon. Nobody was hurt and his vehicle was not damaged. Sidney called police from a gas station. Again, nobody was caught.

Things were spinning so out of control it was becoming surreal. A 21-year-old Myrtle Beach man was arrested for impersonating a police officer. During a cab ride to a convenience store, the man allegedly pulled a gun and ordered the driver to go faster, saying he was a federal agent and thus authorized to speed on public roads. At the store, the man said he was looking for a serial killer wanted in connection with 16 missing persons, including Heather Elvis, and demanded that the store turn over surveillance video.

Police were called, and it turned out the man was in the store to buy beer. The man appeared to have been drinking, which he said he wasn't supposed to do while on his medication as he had been diagnosed with bipolar disorder.

Seeking to relieve the pressure, Horry County Police Chief Saundra Rhodes sat down with Waccamaw Publishers. In a story that posted on Feb. 6, she sought to assure the public that the case was "very active," involving a task force of some 15 investigators from local, state and federal agencies.

"As a mother, obviously it's important to me," Rhodes said. "When I go home at night, I don't have to wonder why there's an empty chair," Rhodes continued. "I would like to give this community a sense of peace."

She spoke only in vague terms about what all that effort had gotten them. "We feel like we have a good opportunity to solve this case," she said. "We have a few theories. It is not at a standstill. What I don't want is a community fearful of being out at night."

Terry Elvis, in an interview with WMBF-TV that aired Feb. 11, said that while he believed police "are doing their job" it was "not to the best of their ability. Because I haven't seen results, and it's been 47 days." Bill Barrett refused to express remorse. "As a friend of a father that's missing a 20-year old daughter, you do what you have to do sometimes," he told WMBF.

Then WMBF interviewed Sidney Moorer, but the station didn't identify him by name, saying only he was the man who had become the "focus of the social media barrage." Reporter David Klugh knocked on Sidney's door.

"How are you?"

"Fine."

"Listen, a lot of things are being said with respect to this Heather Elvis case. I wanted to give you guys an opportunity, if you'd take it, to talk with us for just a moment about what's being said, where you guys are with this."

"I can't."

"You can't ..."

"I can't."

"Is there a reason?"

"My lawyer and I just can't. I mean I'd rather not."

"How are you all holding up?"

"Um, crappy because people are threatening to kill us, and they're not in jail."

A week and a half later, Sidney filed another police report, claiming a different truck with two men inside pointed a shotgun at him around 1:30 a.m.

Tammy Moorer had reached her limit, yet again. She returned to Facebook:

"Enough is enough and today this family will start filing charges against everyone we possibly can. I will no longer feel sorry for you or let ignorance be your excuse. With that being said, we do NOT owe this to any of you, but here are the FACTS! Sidney cooperated with HCPD from the second he was contacted. He spoke with them on the phone, and voluntarily went over to the offices in Conway to speak with detectives in person. That same day I allowed HCPD to come inside our home to take a look around. They also asked to look through our Mickey camper and I granted them permission."

All of that was true, as the public would later find out. The Moorers had spoken to police and had allowed investigators to search their home and their "Mickey camper," the camper decorated with Disney paraphernalia they took on road trips to Disney World. They had, in short, done everything police had asked of them.

Everything, authorities would claim, except one important thing: Tell the truth.

8.

It was a cold, gray Friday morning, Feb. 21, with thunderstorms in the forecast.

The initial media blast by police was short and cryptic: a search warrant was executed at an address on Highway 814 just off Highway 544 Friday morning.

"Sidney Moorer, 37, lives at that address," News13 posted on Twitter, citing the original police report involving Heather Elvis' disappearance. "News13 has a crew on the way to the scene and will have more on this developing story as soon as it becomes available."

Once the news vans arrived, there was little to see. "Our reporters are not being allowed very close to the scene," WPDE complained.

Neighbors had become accustomed to seeing police cars pull up the long driveway because of the multiple calls of harassment, though nothing like this. Barriers went up on Highway 814 to make way for a convoy of official cars from the Horry County Police Department, the State Law Enforcement Division, the Highway Patrol, the U.S. Marshal's Service, and the Horry County Solicitor's Office.

Word began to sweep the community and a crowd gathered outside the house, many of them supporters of the Elvis family, including Jennifer Garrett, wife of Bill Garrett, who was spotted by a Waccamaw Publisher reporter weeping as police swarmed the property. "I got here as soon as I could to see for myself that this was happening," she told the outlet. "It's awesome. I knew the day would come—I was hoping sooner than later—but I knew our Horry County police were on it and doing everything that they could do."

By 10 a.m., according to the Find Heather Elvis Facebook page: "We are in constant prayer today and ask that you keep us and those who are working so hard to find answers in your prayers today also. God please continue to hear our cries for justice and mercy, thank you for your grace on those who seek your face."

The official word came. "The search warrant was executed in an attempt to identify potential evidence based on new information obtained through expert analysis of previously seized surveillance tapes in the area along with financial discrepancies filed with the State of South Carolina on behalf of the occupants of the residence. At this time at least two individuals have been taken into custody. No names or charges are available at this time."

In an interview, the police spokesman did confirm those arrested were Sidney and Tammy Moorer. It was the first time any official had uttered their names publicly.

WMBF, which despite blanket reporting had until now kept the pair anonymous, added for its viewers that Sidney was the same man "who has been targeted on social media for his supposed involvement with Heather Elvis."

Police reports would later describe the scene. The house was a mess inside and out. In the kitchen, according to a police report, "some sort of meat" sat on an island "aged for some time." Moldy potatoes shared space on the countertops with trash. Clothes, toys and trash littered the children's rooms. Animal feces covered the ground in the backyard.

In the master bedroom, the entire Moorer family— Sidney, Tammy and their three children, ages 8, 12 and 14— were sound asleep. One person snoozed in big chair, others on mattresses tossed at the foot of the bed and in a closet. A pistol sat on a nightstand. Two shotguns leaned against a wall.

Tammy and Sidney awoke to the rattle of handcuffs. They were arrested without incident and transported to the J. Reuben Long Detention Center, where Tammy, then 38, was formally booked into custody at 8:50 a.m. and Sidney, 38, at 11 a.m. The children were sent to their grandparents' house. The Moorers' oldest son later complained that officers interrogated him and his sister while their little brother remained in the car. "They started off being nice," he said. "Then they started telling me I was lying about things and I wasn't. I was being very truthful with them."

The Moorers got his-and-her mug shots. They both were wearing orange jail uniforms. Sidney had a goatee, brown hair parted down the middle, blue eyes and straight mouth, no expression. Tammy, by contrast, could have been posing outside the Magic Kingdom for her Facebook page. The camera lights made her blue eyes sparkle. She had a pleasant grin. Detractors would later call it a smirk.

By the next day, Saturday, the arrests had made news across the country and overseas, with Britain's *Daily Mail* giving it extensive coverage. Sidney and Tammy appeared at separate bond hearings where they were formally informed two charges against them: obstruction of justice and indecent exposure.

Sidney wore a bright red Horry County Detention Center jumpsuit. His hands shackled in front of him, his ankles chained, he rattled as he walked. An officer led him to a table in front of a judge. Tammy also had a red jumpsuit. She sat grim-faced, nodding when the judge spoke to her, her blond hair tangled.

With their handcuffs, they both struggled to sign legal documents on clipboards. Sidney didn't say anything at his bond hearing. Tammy complained that she had lost her job "over this."

Judge Dennis Phipps granted Sidney Moorer a $5,000 cash surety bond for the indecent exposure counts, and a

$10,000 cash surety bond for the count of obstruction of justice.

While the charges were serious—the obstruction of justice charge carried a maximum penalty of 10 years in prison, the indecent exposure three years—it didn't escape notice that neither Sidney nor Tammy were charged with kidnapping or murder. The obstruction charged seemed to be linked to the couple's behavior during the investigation into Heather's disappearance.

The indecent exposure charge came out of the blue. Nobody could figure out what it meant.

Asked to clarify, Horry County Solicitor Jimmy Richardson said, "Anything that we release at this point could jeopardize the case. We've got to be really tight-fisted on all of that stuff. Certainly not trying to deprive the public or the family or anyone else of any information, but right now, it could do more harm than it could do good."

Both got lawyers quickly. The chief public defender phoned a local attorney named Greg McCollum, who got to the jail Saturday afternoon to represent Tammy.

"At this stage, I don't know what's happening for sure in the future," McCollum told WMBF-TV, "but I wouldn't be surprised if she or others were charged with a more serious crime."

Sidney and Tammy each posted bond, but their releases were put on hold.

The next day, Sunday, their arrest warrants were released, officially linking Moorers for the first time to Heather Elvis. The warrants said the couple "prevented, impeded or interfered with an investigation to include but not limited to providing and creating false, misleading and/or inaccurate information regarding the disappearance of Heather Elvis and (their) activities in the early morning hours of December 18th, 2013."

The indecent exposure charges related to two incidents between Dec. 17 and Dec. 18, when the Moorers exposed themselves in public places, first at the corner of Atlantic Avenue and Century in the town of Conway, then in the 1300 block of Celebrity Circle in Myrtle Beach. These locations were several miles from Peachtree Landing.

On Monday morning, TV stations broke into regular coverage with a special report. Police Chief Saundra Rhodes appeared at a podium and opened a folder with a prepared statement.

"Good morning," she said. "We want to give you an update on this case. I'm going to start from the beginning for you. On Dec. 19, 2013, Heather Elvis's vehicle was found at Peachtree Landing. On Dec. 20, when she was reported missing by her family, a full investigation was launched by the Horry County Police Department Major Crimes Unit. A seven-agency task force was then formed to investigate the disappearance of Heather Elvis.

"On Feb. 21, as a result of the investigation, a search warrant was conducted at the home of Sidney and Tammy Moorer. Sidney and Tammy Moorer were taken into custody and charged with one count of obstruction of justice and two counts of indecent exposure on the following day. On Feb. 23, both Sidney and Tammy Moorer were charged with kidnapping in connection with the disappearance of Heather Elvis.

"On today's date, Sidney and Tammy Moorer will be charged with the murder of Heather."

She gave the date of the next hearing and said, "We have any questions?"

Hands shot up.

"Could you talk, Chief, a little bit about the indecent exposure charges that started this ball rolling?" a reporter asked.

"I can speak about that." Then she looked at Solicitor Jimmy Richardson. "You want me to speak about that?"

He shook his head.

"Our solicitor does not want me to," she said, and took the next question, which related to what evidence police had to file murder charges.

"We have had some additional evidence that we located during the search that led us to giving us probable cause of the murder charge."

"Inside the Moorers' home?"

"Inside the home and on the property."

"Have you found Heather?"

"No, we have not located Heather. That is something we are still looking for. We're still working on that."

"Are Sidney and Tammy Moorer cooperating with police or are they denying these charges so far?"

"They do have attorneys and so we are working with their attorneys to establish communication at this time."

"Are you searching the property for a body at this point? Where are you looking?"

"We were searching the property for ANY evidence that would lead us to probable cause in this case, a body included."

"Chief, what leads you to murder charges as opposed to Heather Elvis just missing? I'm assuming there was something in that house that indicated a murder had taken place?"

"Obviously, the investigation is still ongoing. We will say that the evidence that we located there led to the charge of murder."

Solicitor Jimmy Richardson said only, "What that evidence is, the combination of evidence that's been put together over the last couple of months, we necessarily have to keep it really tight-fisted at the present time."

What police found, it was later revealed, was an eclectic assortment: Financial papers, six computers, an iPad and iPad mini, several iPods, dozens of CDs, including one marked "A Bug's Life," 13 cell phones, three Xbox 360s, a Nintendo Wii and other computer games, several digital cameras, $10,600 in cash from a safe, and, of all things, a mannequin torso wearing a white tank top.

None of it spoke directly murder or, for that matter, kidnapping. There were no bloodstains or other biological evidence, no items related to Heather. The guns got listed in the police report, but no evidentiary significance was attached to them and they'd later be returned to the Moorers. What police meant by surveillance video and financial irregularities went unexplained.

Later that day, the action moved from the police station to the courthouse. Sidney was brought in first. He wore the red jail jumpsuit, shackled by the ankles and wrists. Tammy, also in the uniform and chains, did the same. They never turned to a courtroom packed with friends and family of Heather Elvis, who were wearing "Break the Silence" T-shirts. Security was beefed up, with officers along the walls of the courtroom as Heather's parents and sister walked in, holding hands.

Sidney now had an attorney, another local lawyer, Kirk Truslow. Tammy had temporary counsel for the hearing.

The judge formally informed them of the new charges: kidnapping and murder.

Neither defendant spoke. Within minutes, the hearing ended, and security whisked Heather's family into another room. Supporters returned to their cars in the packed parking lot, "almost in a daze," WMBF reported, "not believing what they had just heard: Heather was believed to be dead."

The families and the community craved answers. None were coming. Why authorities believed she was dead and where her body might be remained burning questions the prosecutor refused to address.

"We understand and sympathize with the public's desire to know more information about this tragic case," Solicitor Richardson said in a prepared statement. "But the fact remains that while the Moorers have been charged with obstruction of justice, indecent exposure, kidnapping and the murder of Heather Elvis, this investigation is ongoing. In the interest of justice for Heather, her family and friends, and the entire Horry County community, we simply cannot risk jeopardizing either the current investigation or future prosecution at this time."

He added, "The 15th Circuit Solicitor's Office commends the work of the Horry County Police Department and the many different law enforcement agencies who have worked tirelessly in this case. We also appreciate the interest and cooperation of the public as we continue to work together with law enforcement. As soon as we are able to release more information without the risk of jeopardizing either the investigation or prosecution, we will do so, as we know it will help answer questions and provide some degree of closure to a grieving family and community."

After the hearing, community organizers and search volunteers scheduled a prayer vigil for 6:15 that night at Peachtree Landing. "Show the Elvis family that we as a community are praying for them during these difficult times and we and always will be united by Heather," organizers stated in a Facebook post. "As this has been put together today please bring a candle to light tonight in honor of our beautiful Heather as well."

Heather had been missing without a trace for more than two months. The realization that she was probably dead, gone and maybe never to be found was only now starting to sink in. The vigils that had been held to keep up spirits resembled wakes.

"Everyone who didn't even know her is feeling the pain just like the Elvis family," Pastor Daniel Lightsey, who led the vigil, told ABC15. "They're so distraught and so hurt over this, and everybody coming together is helping rebuild."

"Emotions are running wild, and it's kind of hard to describe beyond that," family friend Matt Stoddard told

WMBF. "I don't know about anyone else, but my heart definitely sank."

Terry Elvis seemed to hold onto the tiniest strands of hope. "If Heather is safe and unharmed, I don't care what they do to them," he told ABC News. "They can turn them loose. I really don't care."

Attorneys for the couple insisted there was a simple reason authorities weren't disclosing the evidence: They didn't have any. "Sidney has no connection to, nor knowledge of, any facts surrounding the disappearance of Heather Elvis," Truslow said. "I firmly believe Sidney will be completely exonerated." He would later hedge. "I've not been privy to what they believed to be the evidence," he told the *Post and Courier*, but added that what little evidence he had seen left him unimpressed. "I'm not even sure that you can classify it as evidence," he told the newspaper. "It's more of a theory that they just ran with from the very beginning."

Tammy's attorney, Greg McCollum, struck a similar chord. "To the best of my knowledge, Tammy does not know Heather Elvis at all. I don't think they've ever met," he said. Only later would the public find out that police suspected Sidney Moorer from the very beginning.

9.

For Sidney Moorer, the night of Thursday, Dec. 19, 2013, began with a phone call from Danny Lamar Furr, a corporal with the Horry County Police Department. After Heather Elvis's car was discovered, Furr, a supervisor, went to the Tilted Kilt and spoke with the manager, who told him Heather had not arrived for her shift, which was out of character and concerning. Furr asked the manager if he knew of anyone police should talk to.

He gave Furr the name Sidney Moorer and provided the cell phone number he used for business. The manager told Furr there was "a relationship" between Heather and Sidney with "Sidney possibly knowing where she may be."

Furr called Sidney. A man answered and Furr identified himself. There was a pause.

"Hello?" Furr said.

"Yes."

"Is this Sidney Moorer?"

"Yes."

The corporal told him he was calling in reference to Heather Elvis. "We are currently looking for her and she may or may not be missing and I need your help in reference to this," Furr told him. "I've been to where both of y'all had worked and where she still worked and the manager indicated that you may have some information of where I may find her or how to get touch with her. "

Sidney said he had not spoken with her in at least six weeks. Furr pressed him on how he knew her.

That's when he confirmed that he had talked to her the night she went missing. Sidney said she had called his cell phone. It came as a shock. Sidney said they had a relationship, but were broken up, and now Heather wouldn't leave him alone.

When Furr hung up, he called Officer Casey Canterbury and directed him to go to Sidney Moorer's house to speak with him in person.

As Furr later recalled, "I felt that there was some hesitation in the answers and as stated before I had received one answer about not speaking with her in six weeks and a short time later in the same conversation, I was told that they spoke the night before. Being that things didn't seem to be adding up, I felt a follow-up investigation with the defendant was necessary."

Sidney would later say that the next communication he got was from Terry Elvis, in the form of a text message. Neither Sidney nor Tammy has provided the actual text. But Sidney said after he got it he called 911. The operator said he wouldn't have to wait for police. They were already outside his house.

Canterbury and two other officers arrived at the Moorers' house around 2 a.m. on what was now Friday, Dec. 20, 2013. They parked their cruisers at the end of a long driveway. Sidney came out of the house and met them. Canterbury flipped the record button on his body microphone, which is stashed in a leather pouch in front of his radio.

"How are you?" Canterbury asked. The time code on the recording showed 2:13 a.m.

"I don't know why y'all are here," Sidney said.

The recording quality was poor, much of it inaudible. But Canterbury or another officer could be heard saying police had come to talk to Sidney about Heather Elvis.

"What's your relationship to her?" asked Canterbury.

"There is no relationship," Sidney said. "There *was* a relationship. And I broke it off."

Canterbury asked when Sidney had last been in contact with her.

"I talked to her," Sidney said. "She called me either last night or the night before, I can't remember ... and blew this up."

Sidney handed Canterbury his cell phone, showing where she had called him a number of times the morning of Dec. 18, 2013. There were no outgoing calls to her. Sidney's son later said an officer called Heather from Sidney's phone, but nobody answered.

Sidney insisted he didn't know where she was. Canterbury warned him: "If you know where she's at and you're not telling us and we find out and you're lying about this, if we find that out, you're entering the investigation. We need to find her."

Canterbury told Sidney that police had found 360 texts on Heather's phone from his phone in the last 30 days. Sidney said that couldn't be true. (In fact, it wasn't. Texts would be found, but they were from months earlier.)

Sidney responded by saying something about "my wife is the only person who has my phone." He said, "My wife took my phone." He added, "I'm trying to fix things with my wife. ... I'm not denying it. I'm saying I ended it."

He explained that the family had recently taken a vacation to Disneyland. When they returned at the end of October, "all the shit hit the fan" when he got a call from Heather. "She cried and cried," he said. It wasn't clear from the recording if he were referring to Heather or his wife.

Canterbury asked, "Where were you at Wednesday?"

"I was straightening up in the yard. I worked Wednesday night," he said, guessing it was until 2 a.m. or "something like that."

"Where were you at when she was trying to call you?"

He said he was in the bedroom.

"At any point did you go around Peachtree Landing and there?"

"No."

"There's nothing that's going to show up of you around that area?"

"No."

Canterbury asked if Heather had been seeing anybody else lately.

"All I know is that she dated one of the beer guys at the Tilted Kilt, and that's it," said Sidney.

The conversation ended and the police left.

Heather Elvis had been gone for only about 24 hours at that point. It was still the earliest stages of what might not even turn out to be an investigation at all. For all anybody knew, she was with a friend and not answering her phone.

Later that morning, several police officers went back to the Moorer home. As Tammy Moorer had said on Facebook, she met them at the front door. They didn't have a search warrant, but asked if they could walk around and take photographs. Tammy agreed and signed a consent to search form.

Their cursory look produced no evidence. "I never found anything pertaining to Miss Elvis," Lt. Peter Cestare of the Horry County Police Department would later say.

He would later claim he spotted three video cameras attached to the eaves of the house. As events unfolded, and police narrowed on the Moorers as suspects in Heather's disappearance, surveillance video could have been powerful evidence.

In one of the unexplained loose ends of the investigation, officers never asked Tammy if she had surveillance video recordings from the night of Heather's disappearance. Cestare, whose job was to photograph the house, snapped 27 pictures, but none of the cameras he said he saw. "I did not want to be overly aggressive," he later said in court. The cameras also never made their way into any police reports.

Police were not finished with the Moorers. Later that day, Sidney and Tammy went to the brick M.L. Brown Jr. Public Safety Facility in the town of Conway. They didn't bring a lawyer. They would later say they agreed to talk to investigators in the spirit of cooperation, to do anything they could to help find Heather Elvis, even though they had no idea what happened to her.

Tammy later said in court they first spoke separately to a sergeant named Allen Large, who recorded the interviews and "wanted to see if our stories were different. They were the same." Sidney and Tammy each gave a detailed account of their actions the night before, she said, and even gave the names of stores they visited where Large could obtain corroborating surveillance video.

Not believing them, Large became angry, Tammy claimed. "I wanted to leave. They would not allow us to leave," she said. "Detective Large eventually allowed me to leave the police station when I told him we wanted attorneys. He got physical with Sidney. He said, 'You are not leaving.' There were some dirty words. … He said, 'You're not going anywhere.'"

While Sidney stayed at the station, Tammy drove back to her parents' house. Police cars were parked in front. She had not told her parents yet about Heather Elvis or the police interviews. Before she could warn them, officers were knocking on their door.

Sidney next spoke to two more detectives, Jonathan Martin and Jeff Cauble. From the recording, it appeared that Large may have been present at some point, but he never said anything.

It was now the afternoon of Dec. 20. Heather had not been heard from in more than 48 hours and searchers would soon be scouring the woods and Waccamaw River.

The interview began with the detectives asking Sidney about that last conversation he had with Heather the morning she disappeared. Martin did most of the questioning.

"So she called your cell phone a couple of times, finally gets a hold of you," Martin said. "Where were you at when you got the call?"

"Actually, I think I was sittin' in the bed," said Sidney.

"Were you up still?"

"We hadn't been home long because we had gotten home from work."

"Where do you work?"

"All over the place. I know I worked at Longhorn's that night and I know I worked at Sticky Fingers that night," he said, referring to two well-known restaurants in the Myrtle Beach area.

"What do you do at those places?"

"Restaurant maintenance. Fix broken stuff, you know."

"So you go in places when they're closed?

"Yes."

"Do you work with anybody?"

"Just my wife."

Cauble jumped in. "Was she with you that night?"

"Yes," said Sidney, "ever since me and Heather ended our relationship—well, I ended it—ever since that was ended, my wife found out and all that went on, my wife, she goes to work with me. We do everything together. We don't split up."

Martin asked, "More on her choice?"

"Probably that, too, but, no, we've been trying to work out our differences and get all that straight."

"What's her name?" asked Martin. Sidney gave him Tammy's name and cell phone number.

"So you were together all night?" Martin asked. "What did she do?"

"She just helps me out."

"Do you have a company?"

"I have my own maintenance company."

"So these places you have a pass code to sign in?"

Sidney said it varies. Some restaurants he could go into as long there were at least two other people or a security guard present. Other restaurants he had a passcode. On Wednesday night, he believed the Longhorn's manager let him in.

"I'm trying to remember," he said. But he recalled that at Sticky Fingers, he used an alarm code.

"What time do you think you got finished up there?" asked Martin.

After a pause, Sidney said, "Probably around 1 or so. May have been earlier than that. 12:30 or somewhere around that we left there."

"Did you stay in the city or did you go straight home?"

"We went—I don't want to get graphic with you, either—he's already heard this," Sidney said, apparently gesturing to a third investigator in the room. This may have been Large. When asked later who Sidney was referring to, Cauble and Martin would claim they couldn't remember.

"We're trying to repair our marriage," Sidney continued. "We went to Broadway. We were going to go to one of the clubs if there was a decent amount of people. There was nobody in the parking lot, so we left there, went down—trying to think where I went. I think I got gas at the end of 17 and 10th Avenue there, the one in front of Sam's. I'm almost positive I got a pregnancy test that night. I don't know if it was in that order."

"For your wife?" asked Martin.

"Yes, because we're trying to have a baby."

"Was it at the gas station?"

"No, it was at Walmart actually, in Myrtle Beach."

"Was your wife with you?"

"She was with me the whole time."

"When you got gas, did you pay at the pump?" asked Martin.

Sidney said he paid in cash.

After the gas and Walmart stops, Sidney said, the couple drove down Highway 501 to look at Christmas decorations.

"There is a car and SUV set up like a sleigh and reindeer type thing," he said. "I went and showed her that, and—" Sidney stopped himself and tossed in, "Oh, when we were at Broadway, we had sex in the parking lot. That was the graphic part I was talking about."

"Which side of the parking lot did you park?" asked Martin.

"Like, by the Christmas tree," he said, near the bridge to a Johnny Rockets hamburger restaurant.

"What type of car were you driving?" asked Martin.

"Black F-150," said Sidney. "Then we went to Conway and had sex in a different parking lot."

He struggled to identify the location of the parking lot in the next town over, saying he thought it was in an industrial park near a college and television station and soccer field.

"What time do you think that was?"

"Oh, shoot, probably 2, 2:30 maybe."

"So, then, did you drive straight home or did you go somewhere else?"

"Trying to remember. We left there—seems like I cut over to 544 and went over that way. I'm trying to remember where I went, if I went home then."

There was a pause. "We may have gone home after that. I can't remember."

"And you had spoken to her at about 3 or 4 in the morning?" Martin asked, returning to the Heather Elvis call.

"We were home. My wife was undressed and all. She was in her gown and everything. She was in socks and all."

"Did she know you had gotten that phone call?"

"Yes, she was sittin' there."

"She yelling at you during it?"

"No, she didn't say a word. She listened, let me finish and hang up. It was that. And I told her who it was, and she said, 'What in the hell?' I said I have no idea. So I turned the volume down and put the phone on the nightstand and we had sex again."

Martin said, "If she's not pregnant, she's gonna be."

"I hope," said Sidney. "That's what we were trying."

He said the phone call with Heather lasted three to four minutes. Martin asked when Sidney had talked to her before that.

"Oh, shit, probably, end of October, beginning of November, right around there somewhere." Sidney said it was well before he took a fall vacation with his Tammy and their children, a cross-country road trip to Disneyland in California.

"And it was nothin'," he said. "The last thing that was said or anything was she sent a period to me and that was it. I didn't respond."

The text of a period mark was her way of saying it was over, end of sentence, between them.

"And that was through text messaging or phone calls? Did she normally text or call?"

"Usually it was text."

"Because you can delete them a little easier?"

"That's just the way we usually talked."

"When did your wife find out that that was kind of going on?"

"About the end of October."

"End of October," Martin repeated. Martin asked if Tammy had ever met Heather prior to discovering the affair.

"No."

"Never seen her, never met her?"

"Nope," said Sidney. "The following day, I told my wife what was going on, and my wife actually talked to her and they had planned a meeting. And she"—Heather—"didn't show up for the meeting."

"Where did they plan to meet?"

"I think they were going to meet at Broadway."

"She work there?" Martin said of Heather.

"Yeah," said Sidney. "My wife was just trying to find out exactly what happened. That's all she was trying to find out because I had lied to her."

"How long had you known Heather?"

"Trying to think when I started working at Tilted Kilt. I kind of met her in passing, It was a, 'Hey, how is it going?' type of thing. Sort of like that."

"How did you start the relationship? Just chat?"

"A couple of the girls said, 'Hey, Heather had a dream about you, like a nasty dream about you,' or something. I'm like, okay, good. I'm going about my business. Like, two or three times, that kind of happened. And then we would sort of talk a little more every time, in person. And then she started calling me—and I still don't know how she got my phone number—and she started calling me."

This was in mid-September, he said. Martin asked, "So she started texting and calling and you're calling her back? She's a young, pretty girl."

"Yes, and she was interested."

"Where would you meet her?"

"Usually, if I was, like, working or something like that, she would stop by someplace I was working or whatever and we'd talk for a few minutes. You know, we fooled around a couple of times at Tilted Kilt. We actually had sex in the Broadway parking lot."

"Never anywhere else? Like her apartment?"

"I knew she lived up by the House of Blues somewhere, up that area," he said. "But, no, I had never been there."

Martin asked Sidney why he thought Heather called him out of the blue late Wednesday night.

"I don't really know, to be honest. Because even after I told her to quit calling, she went on for a little while after."

"And this was in October?"

"Right, and then I thought all was well until I got back, and I guess the other night or morning she called again."

Cauble asked, "What was that conversation like?"

"She was like, 'Hey.' I'm like, 'Who's this?' She said, 'Heather.' I said, 'What are you doing?' She said, 'Can you come meet me?' I said, 'No, I told you, I'm trying to fix my marriage. I'm trying to fix what I goofed up.' I said, 'We can't see each other, we can't date, can't do anything.' She said, 'Why you got to be like that?' I said, 'I'm married. I'm happily married. I want to stay that way.' She said, 'Fine, fuck,' and she hung up. And that's when I turned the volume down and then set the phone off. And she called four other times."

Martin asked, "And you just didn't answer?"

"I didn't know. It wasn't ringing."

"Did she say where she was?"

"Nothing. She just said she wanted to meet."

"She didn't say where, like, meet in North Myrtle Beach?" That's where Heather lived.

"No, that was my initial thought: You want me to drive to North Myrtle Beach at 4 o'clock in the morning? Yeah, that's going to fly great with my wife right now."

Cauble asked, "And that was the first conversation you had with her that night?"

"Yes."

Martin asked, "Had you used any other phones that night? Your wife's phone? You make any pay phone calls?"

"Nope," said Sidney. "They still have pay phones?"

That's when Sidney made a big mistake.

Overnight, Martin had put in an expedited request for phone records for Heather's and Sidney's cell phones. Heather's records had arrived electronically shortly before the interview. Sidney's would come later that day.

Martin had reviewed Heather's phone calls and texts and knew Sidney Moorer was lying.

10.

Detective Martin phrased it as a statement, not a question: "There was a phone call made to Heather that night from a pay phone at the gas station on 10th Avenue."

"Okay," said Sidney.

"We have video from that."

"Okay."

"Did you try calling her for a minute, a second?"

"No."

"Are you sure?"

Sidney then said, "Maybe."

"How about we start again?" said Martin.

"I did," Sidney admitted. "I called her from the pay phone."

"Let's start again."

"I know, and the whole story—everything's legit. "

"Let's go back to the part where it stopped being legit."

"I did call her on the pay phone."

"And what did you say?" asked Martin.

"I asked her to please leave me alone because she had been leaving notes on our car when I would be at work."

"When was the last time that happened?"

"Almost the first night we got back from vacation. Well, the first night that I worked, we got back from vacation. I got one on my windshield."

"That was like November or October?"

"That was the beginning of December," he said. He found the note on his truck parked outside Sticky Fingers restaurant. He said the note read: "You need to call me."

"That's it," said Sidney. "There was no signature."

He later got another note one night when he was working at an Olive Garden.

"I threw both away because I didn't want my wife to think I was communicating with her. And that's why I called her that night from the pay phone: Please can you stop. Just stop."

"How long was that conversation?"

"Minute-and-a-half, two minutes

"Four minutes maybe?"

"I guess it could have been four."

Martin knew the exact time and duration of the call from the phone records and knew it came from a Kangaroo Express station on 10th Avenue. The detective invented the part about the video.

Martin said, "It doesn't take four minutes to tell her: Stop, leave me alone."

"I mean, she talked back and said, 'Hey, what's the problem' type thing. I'm, like, just leave me alone, please. I said I know you're leaving notes. I know you've been by my house."

"She was leaving you alone that night. You kind of instigated it."

"That night, yes."

"What prompted that? I mean, you're having sex with your wife. What prompted you to contact her?"

"Because I was trying to stop the whole situation."

Martin told Sidney that police found that Heather was with one of her friends at the time. "I don't know, Stephanie, she's got a bunch of them," said Martin. "She said she got the call and you were talking about wanting to get up with her again because you were going to leave your wife."

Cauble asked, "Where was your wife when you called her?"

"Sittin' in the truck."

Martin asked, "She wasn't sitting next to you?"

"No."

"She saw you on the phone?"

"I don't know if she did or not. She was texting one of her friends."

Cauble asked, "What did you tell your wife you were going to do?"

"I told her I was going into the store real quick."

"Where did you park?" asked Cauble.

"Like, across the street."

"So you didn't park at the store? You parked across the street from the store?" asked Cauble.

"Yeah, like, right across."

Martin asked, "You got gas or you didn't get gas?"

"I did get gas, but I got it at the one at the corner."

"At the other store?"

"Right."

"And then you ran across to a different store and used the phone to call and say leave me alone?" Martin asked.

The interview grew increasingly testy, the detectives' tone more severe.

Cauble said, "You need to start over."

Martin said, "Let's start over."

Cauble said, "Because that ain't flying, boss."

"What do you mean that ain't flying?" asked Sidney.

"Because I can't see you running across the road," said Cauble.

"I was running across Third Street, literally right across the street."

"Why?" asked Martin.

"To use the phone to tell her."

"Why didn't you use your cell phone?" asked Martin.

"Because I didn't want my wife to know I was calling her."

"To tell her to leave you alone? That's what doesn't make sense."

"Me and my wife—" Sidney started to say until Martin interrupted him.

"I think you called her because you were pissed off at your wife about something."

"I haven't been mad at my wife in two months over anything."

"The friend that was sitting next to Heather said you made comments about not wanting to be with your wife anymore. Maybe it was just something you wanted to get off your chest to Heather. That's what she heard. Heather said maybe things will work again."

"I'm not leaving my wife."

"Did you say something like that?"

"I have no intention of leaving my wife."

"So she was confused about what she heard?"

"No, I didn't tell her that."

"You just contacted her from the store phone to say leave me alone?"

"Please leave me alone."

"Where did you go from then? We got a little mixed up."

Sidney was now rattled. "If I'm not mistaken, I think that's when I was going back to—I can't remember if that's when I was going to Broadway."

"With your wife?"

"Right."

"And you had sex in the car?"

"Right. I can't remember why we were going down Seymour Street."

Cauble asked, "What made you think about calling her at that point?"

"Because I had been thinking about notes and shit, and I'm almost 100 percent I had seen her on my road." By that, he explained, he meant the long driveway to his house.

Sidney said, "I wouldn't bet my life on it, but I'm almost positive at least four or five times, I've seen her on my road."

Martin asked, "Were you concerned that she would say something to your wife?"

"It wasn't that. It was weird."

"Obviously, your wife has trust issues with you. She doesn't trust you that much. Is your wife 20?"

"No, she's 41."

"So she's going to be very, very questioning to anything you do from here on out. For you to be with a 20-year-old, she wants to be at your side all the time, 24/7. Are you really okay with that?"

"It's actually not that bad."

"This girl is now—what?—you feel like stalking you?"

"The note thing kind of weirded me out some. I have three children and they play outside all the time. That made me a little nervous. The only time I saw her was at night. And the kids aren't playing on the playground at night. I wasn't worried. It was kind of weird."

Cauble asked if Heather ever wanted Sidney to divorce Tammy.

"She asked a couple times why I didn't leave my wife. I said I loved my wife. I loved my kids. I loved my life the way it is."

"She pressuring you to leave her?" asked Cauble.

"No, not really, I mean she brought it up. She said it a couple of times. There was no like: Why don't you leave your wife so we could do this."

Martin asked, "This was in October?"

"I don't remember when it was. It was just in conversation."

"You said there's been a gap."

"There's been a huge gap. That's why when the officer said last night—and this is what kind of weirded me out, too—that there had been 300-odd text messages between my phone and her phone in the past 30 days, there's no way. Unless my wife's been talking to her. And I doubt very seriously my wife's been talking to her."

"On your phone?"

"Right."

"But she could. She could have your phone or something."

"Well, she has my phone anyway."

"She keeps your phone on her?"

"Yes, and that's fine."

"Did Heather text you that night at all?"

"No."

Martin warned, "That stuff we will find out."

"I'm almost 100 percent sure, I'm willing to bet. I don't have my phone on me, but no."

Cauble asked, "So your wife gives you your phone when you need to make a phone call to somebody?"

"Right, or if it rings, I answer it. If neither one of us recognizes the number, I put it on speaker phone."

Martin asked once again, "I don't see what prompted you to contact her that night out of the blue. I mean, she was going on her normal life."

"I don't know if it's normal life because she had been leaving notes."

"She wasn't leaving notes that night."

"Well maybe not that night, no. It was just an opportunity to try to stop it before it got to the point where it wasn't good. I've seen her in my road. I've seen her."

"What did you do with these notes?"

"I threw them away. I didn't want my wife to know that I had been talking to her."

"What type of car did she drive?"

"Uh, a bluish, silver, I want to say a Dodge."

"Have you ever been in that car?"

"Yes."

"Where would you have been in that car?"

"It was actually just at Broadway," he said, referring to when they had sex in the car.

"Where did you set in the car?"

"I've sat in the front seat once or twice, and the back seat once or twice maybe."

"Has anyone ever been with you guys when you were out and about?"

"No."

"Like maybe one of her girlfriends or something?"

"No."

Cauble asked, "What happened at that point: When Heather started calling and everything? How did the wife feel about that?"

"Well, she was like, why the hell is she still calling?"

"You didn't tell her at that time that you had made a phone call?" Cauble asked.

"She still doesn't know that I made a phone call."

Martin asked, "After that call came in, you at no point left your house that night?"

"No."

"Your truck, nothing? That car never left?"

"No."

Cauble asked, "Did your wife ever leave?"

"Nope."

Martin asked, "She was with you the whole night?"

"Yes," Sidney said. "This is weird, and don't look at me like I'm crazy, like she's crazy, but the trust issue…"

"Yes," said Martin.

"…Is big."

"I can imagine."

"When we go to sleep, I'm handcuffed to the bed. She's the only one with the key."

Martin and Cauble froze.

"She handcuffs you to the bed?" Martin asked.

"That was our agreement for six months. I told you it sounds weird."

There was a pause.

"Which hand does she cuff?" asked Martin.

"I do my left hand, so I can put it under the pillow and lie next to her."

"Okay."

After another long silence, Martin asked, "She handcuffs your left hand. Were you handcuffed when you got that phone call?"

"No, because I was getting ready to go make her something to eat, actually, that night."

"You guys normally stay out late and work late?"

"Not always, but we just happened to be out late that night. We got home and she took a shower and all that stuff and by the time I cooked her food, I think it was probably a quarter to four, four o'clock."

"What did you cook her?"

"Uh, she's on a diet, seems like I did, I probably did pot stickers. She'll eat like three or four pot stickers or something. It was either that or chicken. One or the other. She only eats about three things."

"You cooked the food and then take the position next to the bed and go to sleep?"

"Pretty much, yes."

"You turned your phone off?"

"Well, I turned the volume down and laid it off, on the side table, plugged it in."

"But you never received any more calls from her?"

"Four more after, but I didn't talk to her."

"She know your wife's phone number?"

"I don't think so. She may, I don't know."

"She ever make the statement to you like: Talk to your wife?"

"No, because my wife tried to talk to her, and she didn't want to talk to my wife, I guess, because she didn't meet her. My wife knew everything anyway."

Martin said, "We got someone who says they did meet up at one point and got into a fight or a pushing match."

"Not that I'm aware of," said Sidney. He had a shocked tone to his voice. "No, never. I guess she could know what she looks like, maybe. To my knowledge, they never met, not face to face."

"But you weren't there if it happened."

"It could have happened. Like I said, after my wife found out what was going on, we've been together ever since."

In fact, like the surveillance video of the pay phone, it was another ruse. There was no witness to a pushing match or confrontation.

"Do you think she called her at all and told her stop?"

"They had their one talk. They talked and that was it."

Cauble asked, "Did you hear that conversation?"

"I did not."

"It happened by cell phone, you think?"

"I'm pretty sure, yeah. I think she actually called from my phone. I think Heather called my phone and my wife answered. End of October, beginning of November, something right in there."

"The trip to Walmart did occur?"

"Yes."

Cable said: "We got off there a little bit."

"That's fine," said Sidney.

"You tried to hide little things," said Cauble. "I got to find out which pieces are really there and which aren't."

"There's no arguments that happened between you and your wife?"

"No."

Cauble asked, "Alcohol?"

"My wife had been drinking a little bit, not like stupid drunk or anything."

Martin asked, "Had you been drinking?"

"No."

"What did she drink?"

"To be honest, I don't know what she drank."

"She drink at the house?"

"Straight out at the house."

"Does she drink a lot?"

"No."

Cauble asked, "Did she drink when she came back home that night? When you guys got back home?"

"I don't think so, no, because she had drank two different kinds of liquor and her stomach hurt. We don't drink a lot."

"Where did you drink?"

"She drank at the house before we left. She does it because she's frugal, so if we're going to a club and not have to spend $500 at the bar."

"When you went down and cooked, could she have picked up your phone and made a call to her?"

"I guess she could have. I don't think she would have."

Cauble asked, "Before you guys left to go work, which was at what time?"

"Oh, shoot, I don't know what time we left, probably 9, 9:30."

"At night?" asked Cauble.

"Somewhere around there."

Martin asked, "And you got home probably around 2, 3?"

"Somewhere around that. I knew we had to be at Longhorn before 10 o'clock, because once they lock the door, they can't let me in. And if I leave, I can't go back in. Some of the managers are flexible, most are not, because they can get fired for it."

"You obviously knew Heather," said Martin. "Where do you think she is right now?"

"To be honest, I don't know. I know that one time before, she went to North Carolina. I don't know if she went with somebody or she went by herself or what happened. Her phone was turned off. I don't know how long it was."

"When was it?"

"I cannot remember for the life of me, but I remember somebody asking me at the Tilted Kilt, 'Have you seen her or heard from her?' And I told them this, 'No, I hadn't heard anything, why?' And they're like, 'Well, she didn't show up for work and nobody can get in touch with her and her parents are looking for her now.' Then when I did talk to her, I said, 'Have you talked to anybody else because they're looking for you?' She said, 'Yeah, I called my dad.' I'm like: 'Okay, fine.' We left it at that. I said, 'What in the hell happened?' And she goes, 'Well, I had to go clear my head.' Like, I don't know where she went or what she did or who she was with."

"Have you heard anything about her car being found?"

"Not until I guess it was yesterday when the police were called."

"Do you know where it was found?"

"I think he told me Peachtree Landing."

"You ever been to Peachtree Landing?"

"Yeah, a hundred times."

"One hundred times? You fish there?"

"Fish and a friend of mine's got a boat. We put it in there a couple times."

"When was the last time you were there?"

"A year ago maybe. I don't know, it's been awhile. It could have been two years ago. To be honest, I don't know. It's been awhile."

"Has your wife ever been there with you?"

"Yeah, but that's been a really long time. Ten years ago, probably."

By now it was 4:18 p.m. and the interview was winding up. Sidney was asked about relatives on his property. He said his three children, mother-in-law and father-in-law. The night in question, he said, his wife's sister watched their children at his in-law's house next door.

Martin asked, "When you come home, do you pick the kids up or is it just like come get them the next morning?"

"Usually, we get them in the morning. Trying to think if we brought them home. Seems like we brought them home that night because my sons had exams all week."

"How old are they?"

"Fourteen, 12, and 8."

He was asked again if his wife made any calls during the night they were driving around.

"She was talking to a friend of hers. I don't know who it was," he said. "It was just random stuff."

"Did you talk to anyone else that night on your phone?"

"I think my wife was just on my phone."

"You don't know her friend's name?"

"No, I don't know who it was." He said she talked on his phone to keep the conversation private. Her phone was hooked to the Bluetooth system in the truck and would have come over the speakers.

The detectives said they needed to step out to confer, but before they did, Cauble asked, "Would you be willing to take a lie detector test?"

"Not without talking to a lawyer first," said Sidney, the first time he mentioned an attorney in this interview. "I'll be honest: I don't like confrontation at all. I hate confrontation completely. I get nervous as shit in any confrontation."

Martin said, "It really wouldn't have come up, but you hit something right there, right off the bat that makes me feel uneasy."

"I tell my wife almost everything," Sidney said. "Almost everything. I'm trying to fix what we have slowly gotten back. We drove across country. We talked while the kids were sleeping in the car. We're talking the whole time, trying to work all this crap out. She had a boyfriend and I was goofing around. So we were trying to work all that out.

So that's why I made the phone call without her knowing, just trying so it don't disrupt what we've slowly had taken almost a month to get back to normal."

11.

It was, to say the least, one remarkably eventful night. In Sidney's first account, he and his wife, Tammy, set off in his black Ford F-150 truck from their home at 9:30 p.m. after his wife drank two kinds of liquor to get enough buzz going to keep down a nightclub bar tab. Not trusting him because of his affair with Heather, Tammy stuck close to Sidney on his maintenance job rounds to Longhorn's and Sticky Fingers restaurants around 10 p.m. They swung by a club at Broadway at the Beach, but the lack of cars in the lot suggested a meager crowd, so they made their own fun, parking near the Christmas tree and having sex in the truck. They then drove to the next town over to another parking lot in an industrial park next to a school, and had sex again.

Probably after the truck sex, though possibly before, they drove back into Myrtle Beach, where Sidney gassed up, paying cash, then went to a nearby Walmart/Sam's Club to purchase a pregnancy test for his wife before returning home for another round of sex.

Around 4 a.m., Heather called his cell phone. As his wife lay next to him in the bed, Sidney listened to Heather asking him to meet him. He said he told her no, that a late-night rendezvous would torpedo his efforts to smooth things over with Tammy. After Heather ended the call with a snippy, "Fine, fuck," he turned down the phone volume and had to explain, awkwardly, to his wife who had called. Heather called several more times, but he didn't pick up, not hearing the ringer. That was the last he heard from her. Less than 24 hours later, the cops were at his driveway.

When the detectives confronted him with the made-up surveillance video at the gas station, Sidney changed his story to say that it was, in fact, he who had called Heather while driving around with his wife. He said he parked across the street from a gas station, dashed across 10th Avenue and used the pay phone to implore Heather to leave him alone. He said he did all of this because he didn't want to alert his already suspicious wife, who around this time was sitting in the truck cab chatting to an unknown friend on Sidney's cell phone.

Sidney said the couple then made their way home—they may have had the sex in the truck along the way, he couldn't remember—got the call from Heather, then shut down his phone. He said he made his wife food, maybe three or four pot stickers, was handcuffed to the bed by his distrustful wife, and went to sleep.

The question was how much of any of this was true.

To fact-check his account, detectives had a number of avenues of investigation, thanks to clues Sidney himself provided. The Walmart run would be the easiest to corroborate, for nothing went on at the superstore without it being recorded on the many security cameras. A review of the security footage, obtained by a subpoena, showed that at 1:15 a.m., a big Ford F-150 truck pulled into the parking lot, passed a number of available parking spaces and came to a stop in a handicapped space close to the front door.

A man got out of the truck and was next seen walking into the store past a white Christmas tree toward the pharmacy section. The inside cameras provided a better view of the man: white male in khaki pants, red T-shirt and dark ski cap. He talked to a sales associate, who led him to a shelf just below the pharmacy sign.

At the cash register, another camera showed him pointing to something behind the cashier. She retrieved the item, and he paid for it and another small item with cash. A register receipt time-stamped 1:19 a.m. showed the purchases were an LTL Cigar for $3.63 and an 88-cent pregnancy test. At 1:21 a.m., the truck was seen leaving parking lot.

The pay phone call was made four minutes later, confirmed by Heather's phone records, at 1:25 a.m. The call lasted exactly 4.83 minutes and was traced to a Frontier Communications pay phone on the side of a Kangaroo Express station on the corner of Seaboard Street and 10th Avenue in Myrtle Beach, down the street from the Walmart.

As luck would have it for police, there really was a surveillance camera pointed at the pay phone. Detectives later pulled the footage and saw the blurry image of a person emerging from the bushes and making a call. The quality was too poor to make out the person's identity, but the time code coincided with a call received on Heather's cell phone.

From the phone records alone, it was impossible to ascertain what was discussed in the call. It was also impossible to ascertain who even made the calls. All the records showed were times and numbers.

But four minutes later, at 1:44 a.m., Heather called her roommate, Brianna Warrelmann. When detectives told Sidney that Heather was sitting next to a friend at the time, they were either lying or honestly mistaken about Brianna's whereabouts.

It was a call to Brianna's cell phone while she was out of town. Brianna told police she had left that Monday morning, Dec. 16, 2013, to drive to her hometown in New Jersey during the winter break. Heather was sleeping on the couch as Brianna was going out the door. "Then she woke up just as I was about to leave and begged me not to go because she said she was going to miss her other half," Brianna later said in court, repeating what she told police.

Brianna assured Heather she'd be back in early January. In the meantime, Heather planned to be busy with work at the Tilted Kilt and was scheduled to interview "for a job she was really hoping she would get," said Brianna. They kept in touch by text, phone and Snapchat.

They spoke the next day, Tuesday, by phone and Heather was excited to announce she'd landed the job as makeup artist in a Myrtle Beach salon, having trained for the position and getting her cosmetology license, which police later found in her car. "She was all excited," said Brianna. Heather's mood was also buoyed by a date the next day, Wednesday, with former classmate Stephen Schiraldi.

Then about an hour and 45 minutes after midnight Wednesday, early the morning of Wednesday, Dec. 18, 2013, Brianna got a call from Heather.

"She called me, crying, hysterically crying," Heather later recalled. "When I asked her what was wrong, she didn't want to tell me because she knew that I didn't approve of her relationship with Sidney in the slightest bit."

Heather told her nothing was wrong, and Brianna, who knew Heather well, told her she was lying. "She told me Sidney called, and my exact response was, 'Why did you answer?'"

Phone records showed the call from Heather's phone to Brianna was made at 1:44 a.m., just four minutes after she got a call. According to Brianna, Heather said the number on her caller ID wasn't Sidney's cell phone. It was a number she didn't recognize. Curious, Heather answered it, only to hear Sidney's voice.

Brianna asked what Sidney wanted. "She said that he left his wife and that he wanted to see her and be with her and missed her," Brianna recalled. "I said, 'Don't do it. You've been doing so good. You've been finally moving on. You went on a date.'"

What got Heather so upset was the timing of Sidney's call. "She was mad and she was scared," said Brianna. "She said she didn't understand how he called literally right after Stephen left. Why then?"

For Heather, it brought back the pain of her breakup with Sidney shortly after Thanksgiving. "She was upset and she was hurt because she felt like she loved Sidney. She didn't understand when she was finally getting her life together, why then? Why call then?"

Trying to change the subject, Brianna then asked how the date went with Stephen. "She said that she learned how to drive a stick, which she knew would make me proud," Brianna recalled. "I said, 'Now you can drive my car,' because I didn't want her to burn out the clutch in my car, so I told her she had to learn it somewhere else first."

Brianna asked Heather if she planned to see Stephen again, and Heather said they were to talk the next day when he got off work. "So at this point in time, she started to cheer up and change her mood," said Brianna. "I asked her if she knew what they were supposed to do. She said no, but she was just excited to spend some time with him."

With Heather now feeling better, Brianna returned to the subject of Sidney. "I said, 'Are you going to see him?'— talking about Sidney—and she told me she was going to sleep on it and not make any rash decisions and that she would talk to me in the morning and that she loved me and that was the end of the conversation."

Brianna hung up. It was the last time she would hear Heather's voice.

The phone records obtained by Martin suggested that Heather did not follow Brianna's advice. About 40 minutes after talking to her roommate, at 2:29 a.m., a call went from Heather's phone to the pay phone. Thirty seconds later, another call went out. Then another, then another -- nine calls in all, as if Heather were desperately trying to reach Sidney. None of the calls was answered.

Then at 3:16 a.m., a call went from Heather's phone to Sidney's cell phone. It appeared this call, too, wasn't answered. A minute later, her phone made another call to his, and this time, there was a call lasting 4:15 minutes.

It was around the time that Sidney claimed he was home and got Heather's call.

Eight minutes later, according to the records, Heather's phone made the first of four more calls to Sidney's phone, none of them answered.

The last call to his number was at 3:41 a.m. It, too, wasn't answered.

Comparing the phone records and Brianna's account with what Sidney said gave detectives serious cause for suspicion. The lying about the pay phone call was the big red flag, but there were others. For one, Sidney's memory seemed to suffer lapses at convenient times. That Sidney would suffer memory problems at all struck detectives as most suspicious. All this happened only two days earlier.

Although he fumbled on the pay phone call, some of his statements could be construed as designed to protect himself. For instance, confirming he had been in Heather's car could explain away trace evidence of him in the Dodge if it turned up (it never did). His vagueness about the sequence of events—he was uncertain when he had sex with his wife in the truck, whether he got gas before or after the Walmart run, when they got their children from his sister-in-law next door—could insulate him from further allegations of lying if other evidence and witnesses gave different accounts.

More important, police had to wonder about his anecdote about Heather's previous disappearing act to North Carolina. He, again, was noticeably vague on the details, such as when she took off and where he thought she had been. It was a helpful story for him, though authorities would never produce evidence it was true.

The truck sex admissions simply seemed strange. Although Sidney could have brought it up to illustrate how strong his marriage was, it did leave detectives wondering if he said this as a cover to explain why the Moorers were driving all over Myrtle Beach that night, a route that would have taken them near Heather's work at the Tilted Kilt.

Had they been looking for her?

The detectives had talked to Sidney for about 40 minutes. After a couple of more follow-up questions with Sidney, the interview ended, and he was allowed to go home.

To build a case that would stick, police needed to know a lot more about Sidney and Tammy Moorer.

12.

They didn't seem to have a care in the world. "Going to pick up our camper!" Tammy Moorer announced on May 14, 2013, on Facebook. Preparations for a big trip to Disney World in Florida were in full swing. Her daughter's American Girl dolls had been dressed as Disney princesses. Reservations were made at Disney's Fort Wilderness campground. A budget had been established. Camping would save them more than $1,000 in hotels. And they'd camp in style. Sidney and Tammy had thoroughly Disney-fied the camper with a Mickey Mouse-shaped mirror, Mickey shower curtain, a big Mickey doll tucked in the main bed, Minnie Mouse pot holders over the sink, Disney stickers on the bunk bed, and a Disney Hollywood Studios movie clapper decorating the wall.

These were the days before Sidney's affair with Heather Elvis, Tammy's social media showing a parallel world.

The Moorers arrived at the Lake Buena Vista, Fla., in late May and over the next week and a half, Tammy posted a stream of photos: the food, the children, the barbecues, Sidney setting the outdoor table under a tarp, the bus ride at Animal Kingdom, Sidney downing cheesecake and crème brulée, a fork in each hand ready to dig in. "Sidney Moorer is a pig!" Tammy wrote. There was Sidney outside a London phone booth, his daughter inside pressing her face against the glass, and Sidney posing inside Bell's Cottage from "Beauty and the Beast."

After 10 glorious days, they returned to Myrtle Beach in June and immediately started planning another trip back. "Counting the days," Tammy wrote, adding pictures of the theme park, Mickey cups, Disney-themed silverware and a Minnie Mouse duvet from Ikea for the camper.

While Tammy kept busy posting and planning, Sidney went back to work with a new client: the Tilted Kilt. If Tammy had any inkling of her husband's brewing interest the pretty, young hostess, it didn't reveal itself on Facebook. Tammy projected the image of a family of joy, love and activity. There was the family beach trip over Fourth of July, then a picture of Sidney holding a three-foot long black non-poisonous snake he found while cleaning the yard.

On the same day Heather Elvis told her Twitter followers she wanted to have her way with the man who builds things at work, Tammy told her followers about finding a new home for a bull/boxer puppy they found. "Her new mom and dad named her Luna," Tammy wrote on July 8.

Around the time that Sidney and Heather were having sex on the Tilted Kilt patio and in the parking lot of Broadway at the Beach, Tammy congratulated herself on losing some weight. "I finally ordered myself some new clothes. Being the mother of three, this is something I rarely do. Now, if I can talk myself into keeping some of them, I'll be set." She later suggested the best way for women to lose weight is to pull weeds, "The more weeds you pick the more you lose, and you get a bonus too…a really tight booty. If you're interested I have a lot of weeds that need pulling, just sayin'."

On July 28, the day that Heather announced to her social media audience she was "in a relationship," Tammy expressed her love for Sidney, writing on Facebook, "Missing my long haired, sexy, tattooed hunk of a hubby."

August brought another Moorer family trip to Florida in the camper, this time to Epcot and Disney World, arriving at the Ford Wilderness campground on Aug. 17 after a 13-hour drive. Tammy announced it by posting pictures of their three rabbits with an app that outfitted them with Disneyland Mickey Mouse ears and a Merlin hat from Fantasia.

They took a side trip to Gatorland—the kids held an actual alligator—then it was homeschooling in the camper, with the first day of school. Tammy took a bike ride around the campground and saw a deer, squirrel, rabbit and snake. On Aug. 19, they hit Disney World, riding Big Thunder Railroad.

Sidney was photographed in camouflage shorts and T-shirt standing next to Belle. They watched the electrical parade, and shopped for Disney-themed Halloween gear. Then it was on to Sea World, then back to Disney World, where Tammy posted while on the Haunted Mansion and Pirates of the Caribbean rides. They played mini-golf and ate chocolate chip cookies, pepperoni pizza, popcorn chicken, chocolate dipped ice cream cones at McDonald's. Tammy memorialized the trip by posting more than 100 photos.

After returning home in mid-September, Sidney turned on the charm at home, treating Tammy to French toast with berries. "I think Sidney loves me," she wrote. Tammy wasn't the only one. Three days later, Heather posted on Twitter, "Once upon a time, an angel and a devil fell in love. It did not end well."

October for the Moorers meant more pictures of family and pets, photos from a getaway to Mount Pleasant, Sullivan's Island and Folly Beach—Sidney was pictured holding cold drinks with his son in front of the Red and White Food Store. Days later, she posted a photo of herself with Sidney, both smiling, his goateed chin pressed against her head, his hair long just as Tammy liked it. There was no caption, no message. Just a couple appearing in love.

Two weeks later, she announced that she had lost 20 pounds—"I feel wonderful," she wrote—and on Nov. 21, the family was on the road again headed to Disneyland. "Atlanta is coming up! I am already bored out of my mind and sleepy," she wrote. "Lord help me on tomorrow's 18 hour drive! Oh, it's raining…blah."

After checking in from Atlanta and Alabama, she posted a selfie of her with Sidney, announcing, "Ready to see that Memphis sign," followed by daily updates from Mississippi, Arkansas, Oklahoma, Texas, New Mexico, Arizona, and Las Vegas, where Tammy on Nov. 25 snapped a picture of somebody in a Mickey Mouse costume next to an escalator. By Nov. 28, they had arrived in California, with a visit to the Santa Monica pier—Tammy said she used her handicapped license plate to get a good parking space (she had suffered a severe foot injury as a child in a lawn mower accident)—the Viper Room in Hollywood where the actor River Phoenix collapsed and died on the sidewalk in 1993 ("Had to see it," she wrote.), a Ferrari/Maserati dealership in Beverly Hills, an In-and-Out burger in Huntington Beach, and, on Nov. 29, check-in at the Disneyland Hotel: "Finally! The mouse!"

Next came a flurry of Disney-related posts, Tammy's opinion favorable of the Anaheim version. "Didn't expect Disneyland to be this drastically different," she wrote. "My gazebo in the outdoor kitchen is the size of sleeping beauty's castle! Wow! The new GAC is fine though. Haven't even needed a fastpass yet and the crowds are like Christmas Day in wdw."

By Dec. 7, they were back on the road for home, with posts from Arizona, Texas, Alabama—"Back on my eastern time zone!!!! The east coast the most!!!" she wrote. "I am so ready to see my house! I've missed it so much. Longest vacation ever is over in approximately 22 hours." And on Dec. 12, she posted her first back-home photo: a picture of a Harvey seatbelt back with a design from "The Nightmare Before Christmas" characters.

From a police standpoint, the posts confirmed what Sidney had said about the family taking a vacation in the weeks after the breakup with Heather, with he and Tammy very much back together. Nothing appeared on Tammy's social media to suggest she was angry with him or suspicious. If she were handcuffing him to the bed, she certainly didn't share it with her Facebook followers.

But a subpoena of Sidney and Tammy's phone and computer records painted a different picture than the one on Facebook.

Sidney told police that Tammy had discovered the affair in late October and then had some sort of conversation with Heather at the end of October or the beginning of November. He claimed to not have overheard the conversation or seen any texts.

Using forensic software, police were able to extract large portions of text messages sent back and forth between Heather's phone and Sidney's phone. One exchange in particular stood out. It happened in the early morning hours of Nov. 2, 2013.

It began with a message sent from Heather's phone.

"Sidney"

"Yeah?" popped up a reply. "Wassup. Who the fuck is this. Why would you fucking text at 12:30 and not respond?"

There was no immediate response from Heather's phone.

"Someone's about to get their ass beat down. You bitch is about to take (a) last breath."

Heather's phone finally responded. "What in the world?"

This sounded nothing like Sidney.

"Sorry," Heather's phone messaged back. "My phone was fucking up all night. Wouldn't let me answer calls. And then it just froze. But you've got some explaining to do."

"Why is that? Who is this?" came the message from Sidney's phone. "I frown upon people who hang up on me. Not cool. You can tell me who you are right or I can find out another way. That way won't have a good turnout for you."

"Nobody you need to worry about anymore."

"You want to call me right now to explain yourself. It would be the wisest thing to do.

I've been having Sidney followed since January 2012. It's best you call back and speak immediately. Save yourself. I'll give you one last chance to answer me before we meet in person. Only one. Hey sweetie you ready to meet the Mrs. The kids want to meet you."

"So when does Sidney get his phone back?"

"This is him but we can't talk anymore."

"Can you just call for a minute?" came the message from Heather's phone.

"No, I love family."

"Ha okay."

"Sorry I made a mistake."

"You knew what you were doing. It was no mistake. I understand this can't go on anymore. I just want to know that your wife isn't going to show up at my job. Because I lost hours today because they sent me home after she kept calling."

"She doesn't care about you. She has a boyfriend. She was just mad at me for lying. Wants me to take some tests to make sure I didn't catch anything from you."

"Then why does this have to end if she's got a boyfriend? Stop being such a pushover and letting her control you."

"I can't do it anymore. It's not right."

"Yeah okay."

"You can call if you want. DJ You are silly :)"

"Who's DJ?" came the message from Heather's phone.

"You are DJ. Have you been drinking LOL. Didn't you want to talk? You can call me."

"Ha ha ha. Is that what he told you my name was. I guess you're right. He is a liar."

"Heather, you wanted to speak to me earlier. You can call now. What did you want to talk about?"

"I think you're a little obsessed with me."

"Nah it was a bore."

"If you want to speak to me call me now. Otherwise leave me alone forever."

"My daughter is getting this phone and number."

"Really? So that's why you're still childishly texting me from your cheating husband's phone?"

"Call the number, it's me."

"You call."

"Nah."

"Sidney?"

Sidney's phone ended the conversation with this: "Your skank ass needs to leave me alone. Stop stalking me you crazy fucking whore."

From the context, the majority of the texts—certainly the angry ones—seemed likely to have come from Tammy, who at the time was, according to Sidney, using his phone. Others appeared to come from Sidney. Somewhere in there may have been an actual phone call. Much of the exchange had been deleted off Sidney's phone or uploaded to a computer, and police likely didn't find everything. Nine days later, on Nov. 11, another text exchange caught investigators' attention. This one was between Tammy and her sister, Ashley Caison.

"We are walking around Broadway," Ashley texted Tammy. Ashley said her boyfriend "wants to have a drink at Tilted Kilt."

"Did you tell him?" Tammy replied. "Please don't. Take a pic for me."

"No, we just walked by and had a drink and she wasn't there."

"I think the bitch is in hiding."

While Tammy was going cross-country with Sidney, she sent texts to a friend suggesting that at least during some moments, she was done with him.

"I do not love him," she texted on Dec. 6 while the family was in Anaheim. "He betrayed me and I will never ever forgive or forget it. Trust me, there is zero love on my end. I fucking hate him." The friend's response was not revealed. But Tammy said to her, "It is what it is. I've turned down a lot of hot dick, especially early in the first year of marriage. Truly it doesn't hurt. I fell out of love with him two years ago." The next day, Tammy said things were so bad between them that "Now he had to stay chained to the bed until further notice while I live my life as a single mom."

After Tammy's arrest in February 2014, her sister was interviewed by police and confirmed Tammy was upset about the affair.

"Tammy took more offense to Heather's situation because of the age," Ashley told an officer on Feb. 21, 2014. Tammy had lamented to her sister that Heather was only 5 years older than the Moorers' oldest son.

"Did Tammy tell you about handcuffing Sidney to the bed?" the investigator asked.

"Yes, I'm aware of it."

"He was okay with that?"

"That's what he agreed to. He seemed to be fine. I go over there and seen him even, and I'm really: This is what you want to do?" Ashley said.

"What was Sidney doing?"

"He was in the bedroom. I think he might have been locked to the thing at that time when they were watching TV," said Ashley. "That was Tammy's way of punishing him."

As for the hours around Heather's disappearance, Tammy sent her sister a text, "Home." Ashley had been watching the Moorers' children at their parents' home on the property, and this was Tammy's message they'd be over to pick them up. It was time stamped at 3:10 a.m. Seven minutes later, Heather called Sidney's phone while Sidney was in bed with Tammy.

Of all the data taken from the Moorers' phones and computers, one more stood out. It was a Google search on Dec. 15 for the phases of the moon.

Three days later, Heather Elvis disappeared under a full moon.

13.

Police searched and re-searched Peachtree Landing, Heather's car and the Moorer house and Mickey camper, and couldn't find so much as a speck of blood. Extensive searches of the forests and waterways proved fruitless for any sign of Heather.

They impounded Sidney's Ford F-150 and it, too, appeared completely free of any biological evidence—no blood, no hair, no sign whatsoever that Heather Elvis had been there. Dusting for fingerprints came up negative. They scoured Heather's Dodge, dusting for fingerprints and swabbing for DNA. Again, nothing.

Then police got a tip that they hoped would pay off. A woman who lived on Highway 814 in Myrtle Beach was on Facebook one day when a friend posted a news article about the Heather Elvis case. Through social media, she discovered that a rumored person of interest in the case, Sidney Moore, lived nearby.

She Googled the address and it turned out this person lived just down the street. Having lived there for nearly six years, she knew that the most direct way to get from that person's house to Peachtree Landing was to drive right by her home.

Which was outfitted with a high-tech video surveillance system. Two cameras pointed toward Highway 814.

She pulled the recorded footage from the DVR for Dec. 17 to Dec. 19, 2013. Not sure what to do with it, on Jan. 14,

2014, she sent a message to the Find Heather Elvis Facebook page, which had been soliciting tips. A detective called her back.

Police reviewed the footage. It showed that early the morning of Dec. 18, 2013, a vehicle that looked like a large pickup went by her house toward Peachtree Landing. The time stamp was 4:45 a.m., but the woman explained she had not reset the DVR clock for daylight savings. It was actually 3:45 a.m.

Four minutes after Heather Elvis's phone made its last call to Sidney's phone.

The vehicle could be seen heading toward Mill Pond Road. A right turn there would take the person past a contractor company called D&S Sitework. Police talked to a Sitework representative. The company had five security cameras. One of those recorded a similar-looking vehicle driving toward Peachtree Landing at 3:39 a.m., then returning from that direction seven minutes later at 3:46 a.m.

If manually set, the clocks on both security systems were probably inexact. But they were close enough to convince detectives they had video of Sidney Moorer's truck.

The problem was the video quality. Dark and fuzzy, the images could be of Sidney's F-150, or of somebody else's F-150 or a different model truck altogether. Virtually everybody in rural South Carolina drives a pickup. The resolution was too poor to make out who was in the truck or even how many people.

Ten days after the Moorers were arrested, police conducted an experiment. They drove Sidney's F-150 past those same security cameras at night under similar lighting conditions, then compared the test video with the original footage.

An analysis by the South Carolina Highway Patrol concluded the vehicle in the video was probably a dark 2013 or 2014 Ford F-150 with a moon roof, silver rims, high-end headlights. A total of 82 trucks with those features were registered to drivers in Horry County. One of them was registered to Sidney Moorer.

It wasn't certain, but it was good. Authorities went looking for an outside expert in video analysis for another opinion.

The public knew none of this, the wall of silence having gone back up at the police department and Solicitor's Office after the Moorers' initial court appearances. With officials keeping mum on the evidence against the couple—the police interview with Sidney, Tammy's text messages, her sister's statements all remained under wraps—the community could only wait and wonder and speculate.

So on Feb. 28, much excitement swept the county when people spotted an armada of no fewer than 16 official-looking vehicles head into Peachtree Landing. Police sealed off the area, but from the fringes, people could observe crime scene technicians scouring the parking area around the boat ramp and divers plumbing the brown waters of the Waccamaw.

This sudden show of force fueled speculation that important evidence had been found, perhaps even Heather's body, the hysteria building to the point that the department tried to tamp down expectations. In a rare announcement, police said they were conducting a "forensic reenactment" to determine "tidal flows and patterns" and "grid searches." In the end, nothing came of it all.

The quest for information only caused problems. On Feb. 27, WMBF News anchor Michael Maely went to the home of Tammy's father, William Caison, to get a comment about the allegations against the family.

"Part of our story was about the character of one of the women who is charged with killing Heather Elvis. My duty as a journalist is to seek the truth and all sides and perspectives," Maely later said. "My goal in going there was to give them the chance to respond to some other interviews that suggested information about the character of their sister.

I wanted to give them a chance to respond to that and that was my goal in going there."

In so doing, the Caison family alleged, the newsman ignored some 100 "no trespassing" signs. Tammy's sister, Ashley Caison, later said she started screaming at Maely and told him he needed to go. She claimed he got up on their porch and jammed his foot through the door to keep them from closing it. Police were called and Maely was arrested for investigation of trespassing.

Relations between the media and authorities, already frayed, were reaching a low point. It was part of the larger sour mood in the county. Residents were at each other's throats on social media. Sidney and Tammy's relatives said they feared going outside.

So security was tight on March 17 when the Moorers appeared again in court, this time for a bond hearing. Some 200 people arrived at the courthouse and tensions were at the breaking point between the Moorer and Elvis partisans. Visitors walked through two metal detectors and their purses were searched.

Those who managed to get a seat in Circuit Court Judge Stephen John's courtroom were greeted with a stern warning by the judge. No hats or T-shirts expressing one side or the other in the case. No disruptions at any time. So much as a buzzing cell phone would get somebody tossed in jail.

The Moorers were brought into the courtroom and listened as their attorneys argued they should be released on bond while awaiting trial. Kirk Truslow, representing Sidney, assured the judge the pair would return to face a jury. "If they were going to flee, they would have fled," Truslow said. "If they were going to harm somebody, they would have harmed somebody."

Truslow noted that before this case, Sidney's previous brushes with the criminal justice system were minor. Reporters had done some digging and found that Sidney was involved in two cases.

The first was in September 2009, when he was charged with shoplifting. According to police reports, he stole a CD from a Costco. The case ended with him paying a $210 fine. In 2011, Sidney and Tammy's father got into a scuffle with a neighbor. It even made the local TV news, though the whole thing was treated lightly. WMBF-TV said it "looked like a scene out of a Hollywood movie" that ended with the jailing of a senior citizen, his son-in-law and a middle-aged neighbor.

It seemed a neighbor crossed onto the Caison family property to "investigate" why Tammy's father had "marked off the property line." Things got heated, the old man allegedly attacked the neighbor. Sidney jumped into the fray, and when it was over, nobody was seriously hurt, but all three posed for mug shots wearing red jail jumpsuits.

Charges were dropped and the whole thing appeared to have been forgotten. The smile on Sidney's face in his mug shot was similar to the grin in the pirate picture Tammy posted on Facebook.

Truslow argued that neither of these cases pointed to Sidney as a hardened criminal who'd be a danger to society if let out of jail. If anything, the person most in danger on the outside was Sidney, but he "will take his chances," Truslow said.

As for Tammy, "She doesn't even have a traffic ticket," said her lawyer, Greg McCollum. "She has a strong belief in the courts and looks forward to the point when she can face and answer the charges against her." As a lifelong resident of Horry County, she had deep ties to the community.

It spoke to the tensions in the county that chief of police herself spoke up at a bond hearing. Horry County Police Chief Saundra Rhodes said keeping the Moorers locked up was in everybody's interest during this time of high community anxiety. She said police had gone to the Moorer house at least 39 times, mostly to investigate harassment complaints.

"We were often met by an armed Sidney Moorer. It is my belief that both Tammy and Sidney Moorer are a danger to the community," she said, raising the prospect of "more violent confrontations." Releasing them might "entice a large amount of ill will in the community."

The prosecutor at the hearing, Deputy Solicitor Donna Elder, also showed pictures of the Moorers with guns and noted they had a history of taking long road trips in their camper. What's more, she said, the couple may feel a particular urge to run when they find out how powerful the case was against them.

Then, for the first time, the prosecution presented some of its evidence.

Elder went through the affair between Heather and Sidney, disclosed the cell phone record information with the calls to and from their phones the night she disappeared, and revealed the existence of the security camera footage that showed what appeared to be a truck like Sidney's heading to and from Peachtree Landing. She said the FBI had analyzed it and determined it was one of only a few Ford F-150s in the county like the one Sidney drove.

Her presentation was extensive and detailed and contained several headline-making nuggets. Elder explained how Tammy took extreme steps to rein in Sidney after discovering the affair: taking away his phone and handcuffing him to the bed for six months, both of which a chastened Sidney agreed to. She gave highlights from the angry text messages apparently sent by Tammy to Heather, messages that left Heather "fearful of Tammy," the prosecutor said.

Noticeably missing from Elder's presentation was any hint of how Heather was killed or how her body was disposed of. She said the search continued in the county's waterways with divers and ultrasound.

The defense attorneys would seize on this by countering that the prosecution, lacking eyewitnesses, direct physical evidence like DNA or blood samples, had built its case on the flimsiest of circumstantial evidence, some of which, they implied, might have been fabricated.

The defense attorneys asserted that all the prosecution could show was proof of an extramarital affair and its emotional fallout, but no actual crime. "There is a severe lack of evidence in this case. There is no evidence that he was at the boat landing or in that vehicle," Truslow said. "There is no evidence that he was involved in a murder or kidnapping. There is evidence that he had an affair with a younger woman that ended in October. This thing has snowballed into an outrageous witch hunt, where there is no real evidence."

In his ruling, Judge John noted the "considerable amount of tension and disruption in the community" that left him with "serious concerns about the potential for violence in the community whether caused directly by the Defendant or with him."

"The record indicates that the defendant(s) have a history of travel outside of the State of South Carolina and ties outside the Court's jurisdiction," the judge continued. "The Court also takes into consideration the nature of the crimes alleged and possible sentencing ranges of the charged crimes, all of which raise a significant risk of flight or non-appearance at court."

With that, John denied bond for Sidney and Tammy Moorer.

The audience in the courtroom behaved. To make sure it stayed that way, bailiffs separately released supporters of the Elvis family and the Moorers.

The public had learned in a few short hours more about the case than they got in the previous three months combined. Still, nobody could answer the most important question: Where's Heather?

After the hearing, reporters asked Solicitor Jimmy Richardson just that. His answer was not reassuring. "If we had a body," he said, "maybe we could determine the manner of death. We don't know the manner of death and we may never know the manner of death."

Then a week later, a grisly discovery was made in Florida, not far from Disney World. More human remains. Only these were wrapped in a Mickey Mouse bed sheet.

14.

The city of DeLand calls itself "the Athens of Florida." This comes from the city's 19th century founder, one Henry A. Deland, who paid $1,000 for a plot in what was then largely inaccessible land along the St. John's River.

Until then, the area had had been known mostly for its wild persimmon trees, if it was known at all. DeLand was so flush with excitement about the town's potential to become, as *Floridian* magazine said, "a place of culture, education and beauty," that he came up with the nickname.

It didn't quite work out that way, and today, a more apt description is the city's other motto, "Gateway to the Beauty of Central Florida."

Of more interest to investigators than DeLand's history is its location. The city sits on the busy Interstate 4 corridor about halfway between Daytona Beach and Orlando. It is an area the Moorers knew well from their many trips to Disney World. Prosecutors said the couple had gone there as recently as January 2014, about three weeks after Heather Elvis disappeared.

Had they taken the most direct route from South Carolina, they would have passed right by DeLand.

The remains were discovered, on March 20, 2014, by an unidentified man. "While cleaning the roadway he observed a garbage bag," a police report said. "Upon moving the bag he discovered it contained what appeared to be human remains." The report placed the exact location as Oak Street north of International Speedway Boulevard, not far from Interstate 4.

The U.S. Justice Department's National Unidentified Missing Persons Data System, or NamUs, reported that could be determined that the remains were "not recognizable," except that they were human, adult, and wrapped in a pink bathrobe, curtains and that bed sheet whose Mickey Mouse image appeared to be homemade.

Police in Horry County might have released more information about the matter, except that the next day, March 21, Judge John issued a gag order barring law enforcement officials and attorneys from saying anything publicly about the Heather Elvis case. It came at the request of prosecutors.

"The State recognizes that this case has received and is expected to continue to receive local and possible national media interest," according to the official request filed by Senior Assistant Solicitor Donna Elder. "The State submits that extrajudicial statements to the media, by either party could jeopardize the fair administration of justice in this case." Why the judge approved of it went unexplained, since any outside-of-court comments would have fallen under that very gag order.

Now the only details could come from Volusia County, Fla. Officials said it would take weeks before test results would be completed. Even then, a spokesman for Volusia Sheriff's Office said the remains may be subjected to additional tests.

It meant another cruel waiting game for the Elvis family, already in shock from having their daughter's affair, and other evidence, bared at the hearing. "I once was different, I once could understand, I once could live life and smile," Terry Elvis wrote on Facebook on March 18, two days earlier. "But, then it happened, you vanished, my life was turned upside down, I still do not know where to turn to, suddenly everything changed, still thru it all, one thing remains constant, Heather my dear sweet child, no matter how long it takes, no matter the cost or the sacrifice, I your father and the rest of your family and your friends will never give up hope, we will never give up faith and we will never stop looking for you till we bring you home."

The Moorer family also was reeling. On March 24, Tammy's father, William Caison, died of a heart attack. The family blamed the stress from the case for his death. If they thought they would get sympathy, they were mistaken.

Not long after Caison's death, pictures of him, Sidney, Tammy were tacked to a stop sign near a bait and tackle shop. A red "X" was drawn over William's face. Scrawled on the sign, "One down. Rot in hell."

Another sign turned up showing Tammy with a bullet hole on her forehead. A witness told police he saw a man driving a white SUV that appeared to be a Cadillac Escalade hanging the sign, but nobody would ever be arrested.

"It's hard for me to go out," Tammy's mother, Polly, told the *Myrtle Beach Sun News*. "It's hard for me to go to sleep. You don't ever know who might pull a gun on you. We don't trust anybody anymore. You don't know who you can trust. It's terrible. It's like living a nightmare."

Tammy's eldest son would later blame Terry Elvis for setting the tone. "A gag order was placed on my mom and dad so they couldn't speak the truth when the police stated how many calls were made to them about my family being threatened and harassed?" he asked in a Facebook post. "The calls were made because HCPD told us to call every time Terry or one of the people supporting him showed up. The HCPD was given video, photographs, text messages, and never did they do one thing to him."

Against this backdrop, Tammy's attorney made a request certain to anger a large portion of the population: a second bid for a bond. "The Defendant requests that this Honorable Court hear new and substantial grounds for relief relating to the denial of bond and hear grounds forming a basis of the immediate necessity," Greg McCollum wrote in a motion.

At the May 23 hearing, all rules of decorum were ruthlessly enforced. "Inside the courtroom, a man sitting among Elvis supporters had his cell phone confiscated for taking photos before the hearing," Waccamaw Publishers reported. "At least one other man was ejected for unspecified reasons."

At the hearing, McCollum reiterated what he called the weakness of the prosecution case, particularly against his client. "There's a misconception and misbelief about the lack of evidence against Tammy Moorer," he said. "There's been a lot of speculation that they found forensic evidence, that they've found a hair sample or a tissue. That's absolutely not true. There's no evidence to link Tammy Moorer to the disappearance or possible death of Heather Elvis."

McCollum suggested that Tammy was arrested only to pressure her to turn on her husband or incriminate herself, a contention Senior Assistant Solicitor Donna Elder disputed, saying that there was no rush to judgment as charges weren't filed until a full two months after Heather went missing. "This is a case where law enforcement, contrary to public pressure, they waited," she said.

Clearly bristling under the gag order, Tammy at one point blurted out, "Excuse me, but can I say something?"

"No, ma'am," the judge said.

After whispering to McCollum, her lawyer said that Tammy wanted to complain about the conditions at the J. Reuben Long jail, which she said was overrun with bed bugs and where she said she was locked up with people with herpes and HIV.

In a surprise announcement, McCollum explained why Tammy was particularly sensitive to her treatment.

"The evidence that we presented in court is that she's been examined at two different hospitals by two different doctors by two different medical staffs and they both say that she's pregnant and we believe that to be true," said McCollum. "She's had some problems that we presented in court and that was our concern and we were very hopeful that based on that and the other things we presented that the judge would modify the conditions." The lawyer said Tammy was "trying to get pregnant prior to her arrest" and was now in her second trimester.

Elder wasn't buying it. She said that Tammy had turned down taking prenatal vitamins and other medical attention, including an examination by an OB-GYN, offered by the jail. "I do not believe it is a foregone conclusion that she has a viable pregnancy," Elder said.

Judge John said that, for now, he'd accept what Tammy said as true. He ordered her health be monitored and that any changes—or her refusal to accept care—be documented. "I want that noted in the record," he said. "It will be documented in writing." But it didn't factor into whether he would reverse his previous decision. Pregnant or not, Tammy would remain jail without bond.

Somebody then started crying in the audience section of the courtroom, and after spectators were released, tears turned to harsh words in the parking lot. As rivals traded loud insults, court security officers swooped in to break up the crowd.

Afterwards, two more related legal matters were cleared up. The first was the dismissal of obstruction of justice charge against Garrett Ryan. He was the man police said interfered with the investigation. When the preliminary hearing rolled around, a key witness—a police officer—didn't show up. The prosecutor said the cop thought the hearing had been postponed; what gave him that impression wasn't disclosed. The case was dismissed.

Charges against the other man, Elvis family friend William Barrett, remained pending, though no court date had been set. Both could be revisited, the Solicitor's Office said, but at this point, prosecutors had more important matters to attend to.

One matter prosecutors did pursue, however, was the case against the TV anchor. Michael Maely enjoyed the full support of his station. "We stand behind Michael's reporting on this story that has affected the community. We are confident that will be proven as the case goes through the judicial system," said WMBF News Director Sarah Miles.

The Solicitor's Office sought to bar reporters from the trial on the grounds that any information would violate the gag order in the Heather Elvis case. One of Maely's lawyers, who also represented the South Carolina Press Association, called the state's request "beyond absurd," and the judge agreed.

In the Oct. 10 date trial, Maely testified in his own defense, telling the jury of five women and one man that he went to the Caisons' home on Feb. 27, 2014, for the sole reason of being fair to them. "Their relatives are charged with murder in one of the biggest cases in the county and possibly the country," Maely said. "We have a duty to pursue the truth and obtain information."

He never saw any of the 100 trespassing signs cited by the Caison family. Testimony suggested the reason was because they didn't exist. A neighbor said she never saw signs that day, but did watch as Maely went to the front porch. "I thought it was pretty gutsy going up there anyway," she said. "He had chutzpah." And the cop who took the report mentioning the signs testified he'd done so over the phone and had never actually been to the property.

After brief deliberations, the jury acquitted Maely. The whole thing took four hours.

Meantime, test results were trickling in on the two sets of remains. The first were those found during the Heather Elvis search back on Dec. 31, 2013, and Jan. 1, 2014. The remains had been initially determined to come from a man, but it wasn't the missing Zack Malinowlski.

They were determined to be those of one David Matthew Mino, age 47, of the Surfside Beach area, whose disappearance on July 4, 2011, never made the news. He had been riding a yellow moped when he went missing; the moped had not been found. Police said they next needed to see if foul play was involved.

The next news concerned those bones found in Florida. The remains got careful scrutiny, with a DNA test and two autopsies by the Volusia County Medical Examiner's Office and University of Florida in Gainesville. Additional DNA results were still pending, but the Volusia County Sheriff's Office believed it had enough information to safely inform the Horry County Police Department the remains were *not* those of Heather Elvis.

Another hunt was under way for the identity of yet another missing person.

As 2014 wound down, it appeared that authorities had all but given up hope of ever finding Heather Elvis, now gone a year. "Criminal Investigations Detectives continue to search for leads on her whereabouts, but all current leads have been exhausted," police spokesman Lt. Raul Denis said in a statement. "It is believed there may be someone out there with information that may lead investigators to her or evidence related to the case."

Those close to Heather had nothing left but prayers. On the one-year anniversary of her disappearance, friends, family, and community members lit candles at Peachtree Landing. There was music and tears.

A new year promised no respite. It would not take too much to read into Lt. Denis' statement to guess that police believed that "someone" was Sidney or Tammy Moorer. But the couple accused of the murder and kidnapping of Sidney's young mistress that moonlit night was done talking.

For they would not only soon be out of jail, they'd be out of Horry County, and out of the state of South Carolina.

15.

Nobody could guess it at the time, but the four-hour trespassing trial of the TV anchorman spoke of setbacks to come for Horry County Solicitor's Office in the biggest, most highly publicized case it had ever seen.

On Jan. 30, defense attorneys appeared with their clients—a noticeably thinner Tammy in blue shirt, black jacket and slacks, Sidney in a dark suit and tie, before a new judge, Judge R. Markley Dennis Jr. The defense attorneys had finally had time to comb through the evidence and were energized. This was a winnable case.

"The case was not solved. It's not a situation where law enforcement was able to solve the case and then go and arrest the individuals who are responsible for it," said Greg McCollum, Tammy Moorer's attorney. "The arrest of them was designed to solve the case and if they had committed a crime, it may have very well worked."

From the earliest moments of the investigation, police had one suspect and one suspect only. What they didn't have was physical evidence or a body. Extensive searches for both came up empty. They had a good case, but not great one, a wobbler when what they needed was a slam dunk, and they thought they could accomplish that, the defense attorneys claimed, by going after Tammy.

She was clearly hurt and decidedly angry with Sidney. He had had a fling with a woman half his age at work, that saddest cliché for a man approaching middle age. If her text messages and sister were to be believed, she didn't love him anymore. She had to handcuff him to bed and confiscate his cell phone to keep out of trouble, and had all but written him out of her life. The cops just needed to help her expedite that process.

"For whatever reason, the prosecutor who previously had this case decided to basically bring shock and awe down on Tammy Moorer," McCollum said. Cops in more than two dozen vehicles stormed into the Moorers' driveway, rousted them out of bed and put the heat on their kids. They then cooked up convoluted charges. In a town that welcomes spring breakers and bikers, the Moorers couldn't have been the first to frolic indecently in a parking lot. They then hoped Tammy would crack and turn on her thickheaded, horny husband.

At the same time, police and prosecutors played a similar game with Sidney. "It was my understanding that the prosecutor believed that Tammy Moorer was the killer and they were trying to get her husband to give a statement against her," McCollum said. "I told her, 'If you say your husband did it, I'm pretty sure you're going to walk out of here.'"

"I was told that," Tammy blurted out during the hearing.

"Ma'am, be quiet," the judge admonished.

"There is no physical evidence; there is no direct evidence," said Truslow. Pronouncements from the prosecutor to the defense that Heather's DNA would be found in the truck fizzled. Truslow said the lab botched the test. The sample didn't come from the truck, it came from Heather's own car.

The prosecution didn't have an FBI video analysis showing that Sidney's truck matched the truck in the surveillance video; the highway patrol did that. The prosecution had that word from a guy who taught some classes at the FBI, a hired gun, private-practice expert from across the country who would, the defense would later suggest, say whatever they wanted him to say for the right fee.

In the end, the defense argued, what the prosecution had was evidence that made Sidney, and to a lesser extent Tammy, look really bad. A tawdry affair. An ill-advised and easily exposed lie about a phone call. Some venomous texts from a spurned wife.

And those phone records. The phone records would be a problem.

But any defense attorney will tell you they'd take "looking bad" and a "problem" over physical evidence, reliable eyewitness testimony and a heartfelt confession, none of which existed here. With neither spouse poised to turn on the other, this case was a ripe target for acquittal.

For these reasons, and the others stated at the previous bond hearing, the defense implored Judge Dennis to set bond. Truslow went so far as to ask for a personal recognizance bond—no money down—unheard of in a murder case. Sidney, he said, had "lost everything" after nearly a year in jail, though the audacity of the request spoke to Truslow's confidence in the defense case.

For his part, McCollum thought Tammy could post a bond as high as $300,000 with the collateral on the family home.

There was a new face at the prosecution table, one the Moorers would get to know and loathe. Nancy Livesay joined the Solicitors Office, her employment funded by a state grant to add violent crimes prosecutors. She was no stranger to murder and armed robbery cases. She also knew McCollum well, going up against him in the well-publicized case of one Theresa McCracken-Hall, accused of shooting her ex-husband near Myrtle Beach in July 2013.

Her impressive credentials notwithstanding, Livesay had little to offer. She denied any malfeasance on the part of the Solicitors Office, but otherwise, "There has been no substantial change in circumstances from that first bond hearing."

Then she said the words that are music to every criminal defense attorney's ears: "We do believe we have substantial circumstantial evidence."

She repeated fears the Moorers, if sprung on bond, would pack up their homeschooled children and hit the road in their Mickey-mobile. She also repeated the community was imperiled with the Moorers on the loose. "They have been very aggressive on social media, when this first thing started," she said. "They were aggressive, arming themselves at their house. I do believe at this point, they are a danger." If any bond were to be set, she argued, it should be high.

Heather's parents both testified, expressing concerns about their family's safety. Debbi Elvis said a no-bond hold would send a message to the Moorers to stop inciting their supporters. Terry said he worried about their other daughter, Heather's younger sister. "We're asking you to continue bond in the amount that it can continue to protect us," Debbi said.

In his ruling, Judge Dennis said he didn't want to get into the evidence—that's what the trial was for—but did need to consider the well-being of the community and the Elvis family.

"I have strong feelings, but I'm required to put those aside," he said. "Because the law says I have to presume absolutely, that both these individuals are innocent, not just not guilty, they are innocent, they didn't do anything and that's the way I have to view them."

He set bond for $100,000 for each, but with heavy restrictions. "I want to set a zone around this family," he said. "I think the five-mile radius will protect them." That meant the Moorers couldn't get within five miles of the Elvis house, which would prove problematic as the Moorers live about five miles from the Elvis's. The judge also ordered that both Sidney and Tammy wear ankle bracelets with GPS tracking.

Obviously anticipating blowback, Dennis said the Constitution offered him no other choice. "Not withstanding everybody's strong feelings, including the victims', of the guilt of these persons, they're innocent from my perspective today," he said. "I honor and respect that document. I ask each one of you to do that, as difficult as it might be."

Horry County Solicitor Jimmy Richardson tried to put the best spin on the situation. "Today was only about whether or not they were a flight risk and a danger to the community," Richardson stated. "We had discussed the possibility of a bond with the family beforehand. I think Judge Dennis's (decision) was well thought out. Even though we had asked for bond to be denied, we respect his honor's decision."

At 5:45 p.m. that Friday, Tammy walked of jail and was whisked away in a black SUV. Sidney was released the following Monday at 2:10 p.m. and also was driven off in the SUV.

Tammy's mother put up the collateral of her home for both of them. "I think it's about time because I know they are innocent," Polly Caison told the *Sun News*. "I know that for a fact."

16.

Riding a wave of momentum, the lawyers for Sidney and Tammy pushed harder in the spring and summer of 2015. On March 2, with Tammy eager to tell her side of the story, Greg McCollum filed a motion to lift the gag order. The next month, he asked the judge to order the state to return "any and all items" police seized from the Moorers' home. The couple got much of their belongings back, including their guns, but the gag order remained in place.

Then on Aug. 6, Sidney and Tammy made their boldest request yet. In a hearing before Judge Dennis, Sidney Moorer's attorney asked that his client be allowed to leave South Carolina for a job interview in Orlando, Fla.

The publicity and community animosity had become stifling. The Moorers didn't feel safe leaving their home. They continued to complain about men with rifles lurking at the end of their driveway. Social media remained a cesspool of accusations, conspiracy theories and innuendo. Their children were taunted in public.

One scary incident occurred just that month when an apparently drunk woman turned up at their front door at 3 a.m. and demanded to be let inside. He managed to shoo her away and then called police for perhaps the 100th time. Seen on the Moorers' new video security system wandering their property while talking on a cell phone, the woman was later arrested for investigation of driving under the influence with a powerful .16 percent blood alcohol level.

The biggest problem was money. A debt collection agency had filed a civil lawsuit against Sidney, forcing him to pay back a $6,603.32 credit card balance—much of it charged to Toys R Us—plus court costs. Other bills were piling up and legal costs were estimated to run in to the tens of thousands of dollars.

But no restaurant in Horry County would get anywhere near Sidney's cleanup and repair business. "They did want to hire him, but they didn't want all of this media and all of the threats that were coming from people—they were under fake names. They would harass the restaurants," Tammy later complained. "And these employers that you're talking about, certain ones, like Olive Garden, they loved Sidney. He always did a good job for them."

While the terms of their bond forbid them from leaving South Carolina, the judge had given the couple wiggle room, allowing Sidney and Tammy to travel to border states for spotty work if he checked in with home detention officials every two weeks. Now Olive Garden had offered a steadier gig, though farther away. "They liked him so much, the company forwarded him down to Florida," Tammy said.

Sidney's lawyer, Kirk Truslow, argued that since the electronic bracelets strapped to the couple's ankles could monitor them anywhere in the country, authorities could keep tabs on the Moorers as easily in Florida as they could in South Carolina.

Three weeks later, Judge Dennis signed an order allowing the couple to move to Florida. When not working, Sidney would still have to remain under home detention and electronic monitor. Plus, there were additional restrictions. He would have to provide the court with his new address, the name and address of his new employer, and written verification from the company that it had hired him. He would have to check in with home detention officials any time they requested, submit to monthly drug tests, and waive his right to fight extradition from Florida to South Carolina if he violated any of these terms.

Tammy was allowed to go with her husband, conditioned on remaining under home confinement. "The grounds for the motion are that the defendant has found employment in the state of Florida that would permit her to provide for herself and her family," the order states.

The family of five then crammed into the Mickey camper and headed to the Sunshine State. To save costs, they lived in the camper. While Sidney cleaned Olive Gardens, Tammy returned to homeschooling her two sons and daughter and worked part-time as a waitress, constantly worried somebody would see her ankle electronic bracelet or recognize her from the occasional TV news report. Tammy also took regular urine drug tests.

Over the next months, it was a struggle, Tammy later said, but better than enduring the white-hot hate of Horry County. At the end of 2015, negotiations progressed in the credit card dispute. By March 2016, the couple's attorneys began preparing for trial, bracing for new and damaging evidence to arrive from prosecutors.

Only it never arrived.

Which may explain why, on March 10, 2016, Solicitor Jimmy Richardson announced that his office would drop the murder charges against both of them (along with the indecent exposure charges and an obstruction of justice charge against Tammy).

A mad scramble by reporters for some explanation brought only silence. Citing the gag order, the prosecutor's office declined to comment, as did the police department. Heather's family only said they remained focused on finding their daughter and nothing else.

From the very start, authorities had to cope with the fact they had a no-body homicide, which are not as unusual as one might imagine, according to Thomas A. "Tad" DiBiase, former federal prosecutor and an expert on such cases known in the legal community as the "no-body guy," who has written the leading text, "No-Body Homicide Cases: A Practical Guide to Investigating, Prosecuting, and Winning Cases When the Victim Is Missing."

DiBiase tracked murder cases dating back to the 1830s, and has only found 525 that have gone to trial. Of those, prosecutors have secured convictions 88 percent of the time. It would seem a stunning success rate except that the number is skewed by heavy self-selection. Prosecutors won't go to trial without a body unless they have an extremely strong case.

DiBiase (who was not involved in the Heather Elvis case) says that's because of the many obvious hurdles prosecutors face. The most important evidence is the actual body—it can tell cause and time of death. It can also show how the victim was killed, providing clues that link the murder to a weapon, for instance, and by whom, through DNA and other evidence the attacker may have left on the body.

It used to be a prosecutor wouldn't move forward with murder charges at all without a body. It was too difficult to prove that the victim was dead. For a defense attorney, the biggest argument for reasonable doubt is the possibility the murder "victim" may suddenly walk into the courtroom one day.

Technological advances have changed that. DNA testing is widespread and accepted enough now that prosecutors often can point to blood and other biological evidence found at scene as belonging to the victim, perhaps even comingled with the defendant. Another change is cell phones. "We all leave behind an electronic trail," DiBiase says. Where once police would try to show that a missing person was dead by the fact they didn't use an ATM or a charge card, now they can point to a lack of cell phone usage. Cell phone locations can be tracked and text messages extracted. What's more, with the popularity of social media, anybody who stops tweeting suddenly can be reasonably considered a goner.

Of those more than 500 no-body cases, more than half have been tried in the last 19 years.

The Solicitor's Office originally thought the Heather Elvis case would be one of them. While it didn't have DNA, prosecutors did have all that cell phone and social media evidence, plus the analysis of the surveillance video of the truck heading to Peachtree Landing. What struck DiBiase, however, was how fast authorities moved. They could have sat on the evidence they had, secure in thinking that the Moorers wouldn't flee, and wait for the couple to make a mistake. "My advice would have been do more," he says. "They could have taken more time and develop their evidence a little better. They rushed to get them arrested, and now they're stuck with that."

Sidney Moorer could only gloat. "Horry County prosecutors' have failed!" he proclaimed on Facebook. "They arrested an innocent couple and held them hostage for more than two years. The solicitor got away with ruining their lives and damaging the lives of three young children."

In an interview three weeks later with the *Sun News*, Sidney had tempered his enthusiasm. He noted that while the family was happy, the prosecutor still left open the possibility of refiling the murder charges later. "They've screwed me once. Why wouldn't they do it again," he said. "I mean, they've got the perfect opportunity to do it again for the rest of my life. But this is the problem they'll run into: we didn't commit the crime. Therefore, they will never, ever find any legitimate evidence that we did this."

He would not have to wait long to find out. A trial would begin in less than three months.

17.

It was a Chamber of Commerce morning, the sort that beckons visitors by the millions to Horry County, a warm 76 degrees that would top out at 84 by noon, the overnight clouds giving way to clear, sunny skies with a light breeze, the Southern humidity in check at under 50 percent.

A perfect day for the sand or the golf course. A balmy night beckoned for strolling the restaurants and clubs at The Strand and Broadway at the Beach.

A different atmosphere existed for those packing Courtroom 3B of the Horry County Government and Justice Center: High tension, high stakes, nerves on edge, an invisible wall the only barrier between camps that had been warring online and on the streets for 2½ years.

It had taken five hours to select the jury from a pool of hundreds of prospects culled from 800 summonses, a cross-section of the 333,000 souls of Horry County, waiters and janitors, government workers, retirees and students, and some with no apparent means of support.

In a trial promising to delve into the complexities of the human heart, the passions of the flesh, and violations of the marital vows, prospects were first and foremost asked to provide their current matrimonial status. "Happily divorced," one woman said, and she wasn't alone. Single, divorced, separated. A juror in a blissful union of husband and wife proved elusive. The final panel was winnowed down to 14—12 jurors and two alternates. It tilted steeply male: 10 men and four women.

Judge Dennis, decked out in his lawyerly Southern best in a bowtie peeking out of his robe, admonished the audience to remain on best behavior or incur his wrath with prompt ejection for any transgression from absolute decorum, from an audible cell phone to audible reaction to anything the lawyers or witnesses say.

As was his practice, the judge descended from the bench and stood square in front of the jurors to deliver welcoming remarks and warn them that anything they were about to hear from lawyers was not evidence in the legal sense. The only true evidence would come from the witness stand or the photos and documents that met his approval. He may wear the trappings of a judge, but the final arbiter of truth and justice would be the sole responsibility of the jurors.

With that, on June 20, 2016, opening statements in the case of the People of the State of South Carolina, Horry County, vs. Sidney Moorer commenced. Once prosecutors had intended to try Sidney along with his wife for murdering Heather early that morning at Peachtree Landing. Now, Sidney faced a reduced charge of kidnapping, and would face it alone. United in marriage despite infidelity, arrest and pubic scorn, the Moorers were separated only by the legal system. They would each have their own trials, Tammy's to follow Sidney's.

Martin Spratlin, a prosecutor from the Horry County Solicitor's Office, stood and approached the jury box. The state faced a number of challenges. The biggest problem was how to account for Heather Elvis. It was a no-body homicide that had morphed into a no-body kidnapping case.

"The facts of this case occurred on Dec. 18, 2013," he began. "However, the issues in this case are about as old as man has been on the Earth. See, at its heart, this case is about an affair, an extramarital affair that man had with 20-year-old Heather Elvis."

That man, Spratlin said, sat at the defense table.

Sidney was now 40 years old, but could pass for younger, his face tanned from the Florida sunshine. Life out on bond meant he didn't have the prison pallor that afflicts so many defendants. He arrived at court business casual, in a green shirt, jacket, no tie, with a neatly trimmed goatee. He was still the handsome man Heather fell for.

The judge had also had bifurcated the two charges against Sidney. In this trial, Sidney would only defend himself against the charge of kidnapping. Prosecutors had wanted him tried on both kidnapping and obstruction of justice, arguing that the offenses were interlocked and supported by overlapping witnesses and evidence. The defense had portrayed the offenses, from a legal standpoint, so sufficiently distinct that trying them together would require essentially two trials in one, with the attendant confusion for the jury.

At a pretrial hearing, Judge Dennis sided with the defense. And so now, Spratlin was before a jury with the task of explaining how the state would show how Sidney perpetuated kidnapping on a woman without any physical evidence or eyewitness testimony, including an account from the victim herself, as she had simply vanished.

To do so, Spratlin asked the jury to "picture a small boy on a river, throwing a rock into the river." The rock may sink out of sight, he said, but it would cause "consequences to the water: splash, ripples that come off, little mini-waves."

"In the ordinary cases of an affair, you might think that the consequence would be something along the lines of embarrassment, maybe separation, maybe even a divorce," he continued. "Those would be the ripples you could expect to see from an affair. For 20-year-old Heather Elvis, however, the consequences of her affair with that man were not simply ripples in the water. They were the equivalent of a tidal wave. And you're going to hear that that tidal wave came crashing down on her on the morning of Dec. 18,

2013, when that man, Sidney Moorer, kidnapped her at the Peachtree Boat Landing."

Poetry, this wasn't. The metaphorical mash-up spoke to the challenges the prosecution faced. They couldn't say everything they wanted to. They had a case of a missing woman whom authorities had long since stopped looking for and was presumed dead, yet they couldn't say she was murdered. They couldn't say how they thought she died. They could only build a case of how they thought she came to go missing.

Spratlin next sought to show how a person can be considered legally kidnapped when nobody knew how she was kidnapped or where she even was, or is. The law, he explained, has an expansive definition of kidnapping that may prove counterintuitive to non-lawyers. A victim need not be apprehended by masked men, tied up and tossed into a car, like they are in TV shows and movies. Even tricking, decoying or luring somebody into a confined situation fit the kidnapping criteria, he said.

In this case, according to Spratlin, Heather was lured when Sidney called her from the pay phone to set up a rendezvous at the boat landing. Nobody knows what Heather was thinking, but clearly, abduction wasn't on her mind. Sidney's intent, therefore, was criminal.

It was all theoretical stuff, requiring an attentive jury to draw inferences. As he previewed the rest of the case, retracing Heather and Sidney's affair and its fallout, the phone records, surveillance video, Spratlin returned several times to his watery imagery.

"Going back to my analogy about the boy on the banks of the river," he said, "if that boy didn't want you to see that he threw the rock or know that he threw a rock into the water, he'd try to dust the dirt off hands, get it out of his fingernails. The defendant did the same thing. Anything that he could control, anything that he could do to make sure you didn't know what he did he did, dusted it off as best he could. But he couldn't do anything about the ripples in the water, because that was outside his control. You can't stop the ripples. It's the ripples in the water that will show you that that boy threw that rock in the water, and it's the same ripples in the water that are going to show you that that man, that man right there"—he pointed again to Sidney—"kidnapped Heather Elvis."

It may have been one dip too many in the river, for Spratlin was risking taking an already tricky case and confusing it further. Defense attorney Kirk Truslow wasted little time mocking it.

As he strode up to the jury box, he threw up his arms and said, "Well, what do we need to be here for? We've got it all figured out. Boy threw a rock in the water."

Truslow tried to turn the analogy in a way beneficial to the defense. "You didn't see the boy there with the rock," he said. "How about if you got six boys standing there on the bank. Can you tell me which boy threw the rock based on the ripples if you didn't see it?"

The answer was a resounding no, though by now, the jury could be forgiven if jurors were confused about who was on trial: Sidney Moorer or a kid with a rock.

Truslow at last moved on, taking a second dig at the prosecutor's opening oration. "The longer an opening statement, in my experience—and this is only my experience, I can only speak for myself—the worse and weaker the case," he said. "I didn't want to get you and go through the whole case and try the whole case in an opening statement. And I'm still not going to do that as was just done."

It just wasn't the defense's job to prove Sidney didn't do something; it was the state's burden to prove that he did, beyond a reasonable doubt. "As we go through this trial, I'm going to be straight with you all the way through it," he said. "I'm not a song-and-dance man like we see on TV, and lawyers get a reputation of trying to twist facts and all that. I'm going to give you my solemn vow now there's none of that going on here. This is going to be straight about what happened, straight what the witnesses said, what does it mean. We've got an answer for everything, because he didn't do this."

It was a sharp, concise, classic reasonable doubt opening statement with one glitch. Having equated a windier opening statement to a weaker case, Truslow's remarks timed out at 20 minutes—four minutes longer than the prosecution.

The state opened its case by taking jurors, figuratively, into Heather's place of work. Tilted Kilt manager Jessica Cooke explained Heather's duties as hostess who put in full-time hours, but got part-time benefits. Heather was conscientious, on time. At 20 years old, she was too young to serve alcohol, but she greeted customers with friendly smile and a skimpy uniform, and took them to their tables. The servers took the orders. Sidney, according to Cooke, had been the graveyard shift maintenance man for about six months when he and Heather began a relationship.

"And if you don't mind, tell the jury a little bit about that relationship," asked Nancy Livesay.

"Heather seemed to have a fondness for him," she said of when Sidney first started. "And they started hanging out at the host stand and talking."

"And if you don't mind, tell this jury, would he come in and see her on days he wasn't even working?"

Livesay had a quirk of starting many of her questions with the phrase, "If you don't mind." It came in the beginning: "If you don't mind, tell this jury how old you are?" And went through the testimony: "If you don't mind, tell me how many hours he worked?" It would happen with nearly every witness.

With one noticeable exception. But that would be a different witness, at a different time.

As Cooke recalled, Sidney bringing Heather coffee, the prosecutor asked, "Were there any other men bringing her coffee?"

"No," said Cooke.

"Were there any other men coming in to see her?"

"No."

Cooke recalled sneaking a peek at Heather's phone as it charged in the office and seeing the romantic texts between Heather and Sidney, as well as the "red flag" reference to having sex on the back patio of the restaurant.

"What was your understanding of the relationship?"

"I figured they were seeing each other. I didn't have confirmation until I actually read the text messages in the phone."

"Kind of like boyfriend-girlfriend?

"Yes."

"At any point did that relationship change?"

"It did."

"And if you don't mind, tell the jury about it."

"In October, two of the girls at Tilted Kilt decided to make a prank phone call saying that Sidney's wife had found out. And Heather freaked out. She wanted to leave. She—" Cooke's voice broke and she paused. "I'm sorry, I'm very nervous."

She composed herself and continued. "Somehow, we found out that the girls made the phone call and it wasn't actually Tammy. The employees found out it was two of the girls. After that point, Heather left him and there was no relationship."

This left Heather "very sad" and "kind of upset that the relationship was no longer because she actually had feelings," Cooke said. "It seemed to me that she really had true feelings for him."

Livesay then asked a question that brought the first big surprise of the trial: Had Cooke noticed any physical changes in Heather after the breakup?

Cooke had intimate knowledge of the physique of Heather, as she did all of her employees, since her duties included monitoring the restaurant's uniforms. "She had to change her bra out from an A cup to a B cup and later to a C cup and also needed a bigger kilt," said Cooke. "At first, when she went from the A cup to the B cup, she thought she gained some weight. But then she started to be concerned when she had to go to the C cup and get the bigger kilt."

So concerned that Heather took a pregnancy test in the Tilted Kilt restroom.

"Did you see the pregnancy test?"

"I did."

"And tell the jury what it said."

"It said error. I went and looked up why it said error: either inconclusive or didn't urinate on it enough."

Cooke said that despite the pregnancy scare, Heather went back to her usual bubbly self. The last time she saw Heather was on the Sunday or Monday before she disappeared on that Tuesday night/Wednesday morning.

"Have you heard from her since then?"

"I have not."

"Has there ever been a time before this that she did not just show up at work and nobody heard from her?"

"No, ma'am," said Cooke. "I tried texting her to find out where she was. I don't remember if it was her mom or dad came to work saying nobody had seen her."

Livesay wrapped up her questioning by asking if Cooke had ever seen any pictures on Heather's phone of Sidney.

"Yes, ma'am," said Cooke, and Truslow objected on the grounds the question was irrelevant and prejudicial. The judge overruled the objection and Livesay asked, "Tell this jury the picture you saw on the phone."

"It was a picture of Sidney Moorer performing oral sex on his wife."

"No further questions, your honor."

It was a strong start to the state's case in chief and immediately put the defense on the defensive. The revelation that Heather may have been pregnant was a game changer.

It spoke to motive for kidnapping, or worse, for both Sidney and Tammy.

It also put a new light on Sidney's actions the night of Heather's disappearance. He never gave good answer for why he called Heather right after buying a pregnancy test that he said was for his wife. Was the test for Heather? Had he arranged the rendezvous to confront her, taking Tammy along? Did he tell her to take the test right there? What happened if she refused? Or if it were positive?

Truslow wisely didn't touch any of that. He began cross-examination where Livesay left off, asking, "How did you know the oral sex picture was his wife?"

"That is a good question. I did not see her face."

"Did you clearly see his?"

"Yes."

It was a cringe-worthy exchange, but one that spoke to a key element of the defense. At no time in the case could anyone prove who was actually calling or texting what. Truslow moved on to ask Cooke about two other men in Heather's life, seeking to plant the first seeds of reasonable doubt by suggesting Sidney wasn't the only one who could have wished her harm. One, the lawyer suggested, was a prior boyfriend, the other a coworker. Cooke knew nothing much about either.

Next, Truslow sought to burst the angelic bubble around Heather. Prosecutors would repeatedly cite her age, referring to her as a "girl" or a "young girl" or a "little girl," as if Sidney had snatched her from a junior high school playground.

In fact, as Truslow elicited, Heather was very much a grown woman. Cooke recalled how Heather had slept in her car and then at Cooke's house in the spring of 2013 due to some troubles at home, but she knew little else. And she confirmed that Heather had come to work one day around the time of the breakup with a black eye and a less-than-plausible reason.

"She had given me two stories," said Cooke. "One was that when she opened her door, she hit her eye with the door. The other one was that she had gotten jumped in the Walmart parking lot. She said she had to stab somebody with her knife."

On redirect, Livesay brought it back to the Moorers. Cooke had testified that when he saw Heather's phone, it had 95 texts or calls from one person. Livesay asked what name that person used.

"Crazy Bitch," said Cooke.

"And do you know who that was?"

"Tammy Moorer."

"Who is Tammy Moore?"

"The defendant's wife."

More Tilted Kilt staff came to the stand. Server Jodie Lynn Davenport also talked about the obvious affair between Heather and Sidney and seeing changes in Heather's body.

"She looked like she was putting on some weight in her cheeks," said Davenport, "and I remember she had to go up a couple of bra sizes on her uniform—that that was part of the uniform. She was putting on weight around the hip area and the belly."

"What did you think was going on?" asked Livesay.

"I thought she was pregnant."

Davenport, too, saw the pregnancy test with the error message.

Clearly, there were no secrets among the ladies at the Tilted Kilt, their personal lives as bare as their outfits.

Truslow again dodged the pregnancy issue and instead continued to raise the specter of alternative suspects, asking if Heather had any other boyfriends.

"She wasn't involved with anyone," Davenport said.

"You weren't with her all the time?"

"No, sir."

The next witness, server Megan Bonfert, covered the same ground. She, too, had seen the oral sex picture and noticed Heather's weight gain. "She couldn't get into her jeans and she had gone up a few bra sizes," she said.

"What did you think was going on?" asked Livesay.

"I questioned her and asked her if she was pregnant," said Bonfert.

Rules against hearsay testimony barred her from saying what Heather answered. Bonfert could only state she was aware Heather had taken a pregnancy test.

Livesay asked when was the last time she had seen Heather.

"Dec. 10th at our Christmas party," she said.

The question stabbed at Bonfert. Her voice wavered. Her eyes watered.

"Have you seen her or talked to her since then?"

"No, ma'am," she shuddered.

"Was she scheduled to come into work since then?"

"Yes, ma'am."

"Did she come into work?"

Sniffling, she answered, "No, ma'am."

"How do you know that?"

"I sat and waited to see if she would show up to work and she didn't show up. I kind of knew that something was wrong."

Truslow again chipped away at the prosecution's sunny portrayal of Heather. Bonfert acknowledged that Heather felt like a family outcast, a rebel without a cause.

"A typical teenage girl," said Bonfert.

"She was 20?" noted Truslow

"Yes."

"You think a typical teenage girl is an outcast in her family?"

"Not necessarily an outcast."

"Would you consider her sister an outcast in the family or a rebel without a cause?"

Bonfert answered simply, "No, sir."

It was a cheap shot during a potentially dangerous line of inquiry. The defense can only go so far sullying a victim before the jury takes offense. Truslow pressed the matter one more time. He asked Bonfert how some of the other women at Tilted Kilt felt about Heather having an affair with Sidney. She knew other servers didn't like it. And she told how they expressed themselves with the blackboard message: "Hey, ladies, please stop fucking the maintenance man, he's married."

If there would ever be a witness the defense would torpedo as an alternative suspect, it was the next one. Stephen Schiraldi was soft-spoken, bespectacled, skinny. Schiraldi represented, for the prosecution, the anti-Sidney, the mannered young man who treated Heather with kindness and respect. It was hard not to wonder what would have happened if Heather had begun a relationship with him in the summer of 2013 instead of Sidney.

Stephen spoke of seeing her back in high school, catching up with her years later on Instagram, then "officially meeting" Heather on Dec. 17, 2013, when he picked her up for an evening of Mexican food, driving lessons and movie watching at his house, all ending with a chaste kiss, some text messages, a phone calls, and plans to get together again soon.

A rare moment of levity came to the courtroom when he talked about teaching her how to drive the stick shift.

"How did Heather do driving the truck?" Livesay asked.

"She did pretty well. She picked it up in 20 minutes."

"Didn't burn your clutch out or strip your gears?"

"Thankfully, no," he said with a half smile, eliciting laugher in the courtroom.

He recalled dropping her off at her "typical 20-year-old girl's apartment" at 1:30 a.m. with plans to see her the next day after his chef shift ended.

When he was asked if he had seen her since, his face turned sad and he slowly shook his head. "I have not."

It was poignant moment, immediately shattered by Truslow, who opened cross-examination with a loaded question: "Would you agree with me that you are the last individual to lay eyes on Heather Elvis?"

"To my knowledge, yes."

"Did you share the kiss inside or outside?"

"Outside."

"Was there any talk of you staying any longer than five minutes?"

"No, we were both tired and ready to call it a night."

"Would you, if given an opportunity, stayed any longer?"

"I don't think I would have, no."

"That's on your honor?" the lawyer asked.

"On my honor."

"We're to believe that that is true based upon your word?"

"Yes, sir."

"And nothing else?"

"Yes, sir."

The insinuations were obvious. Schiraldi never lost his composure.

"There's no way that you left the house and followed her around?"

"No, there's not."

"There's no way that you never left her house and stayed outside in your truck?"

"I went home."

"According to you?"

"Yes."

"Do you believe that that could be somewhat suspicious?"

"That I went home?"

"If somebody else was looking at it, does that seem suspicious to you?"

"No, just seemed like a regular night that two people went out on a date and parted ways."

Truslow took one more shot. "Nobody else knows what you were up to, but you?"

"Yes," he said, unflappable to the end.

On redirect, Livesay was determined to point out the contrast between a night with Stephen Schiraldi and a night with Sidney Moorer.

"You did not contact her from a pay phone?"

"No, I did not."

"Do you know if she met someone after you left?"

"I have no idea."

"Did you go to the Peachtree boat landing on Dec. 18, 2013?"

"No."

Stephen served as a strong lead-in to the next set of witnesses, all cops. Casey Guskiewicz recounted finding Heather's Dodge shortly after 4 a.m. "parked awkwardly" at the end of the remote one-way street dead-ending at Peachtree Landing, and explained why he left it there. "It's not uncommon for people to leave their vehicles parked at boat landings overnight or even for extended periods of time," he said under questioning by Spratlin. "It was just a vehicle parked at a boat landing."

Officer Kenneth Canterbury testified about he how found the car parked at the landing later the next night while responding to a call about a suspicious vehicle. He also checked, looked inside and saw nothing more suspicious than a messy interior. When he ran the plate, it came back to the name Terry Elvis, the son of Canterbury's barber. After going to Terry's nearby home to tell him about the car, the pair returned to the landing, where Terry unlocked the vehicle, finding his daughter's driver's license but no purse or cell phone amid the clutter.

After failing to reach Heather on her cell phone, Terry put on gloves and drove the car back to his home while Canterbury contacted her roommate, Brianna Warrelmann, getting her account about an upset Heather speaking the night before to her former lover, Sidney Moorer. Canterbury recalled how he then notified his boss, Cpl. Danny Lamar Furr, who told the jury he went to the Titled Kilt.

"In the conversation with the manager, it was learned that there was a relationship between the defendant and Heather Elvis, and in a further conversation of Sidney Moorer, possibly knowing where Heather Elvis may be," said Furr. "I asked for his phone number, thinking he might have direct information of her whereabouts."

Furr recounted his late-night phone call with Sidney Moorer with the initial pause from Sidney when Furr identified himself as a police officer. "From there, he stated that he had not spoken with her in at least six weeks," Furr told the jury. When Sidney acknowledged he had spoken to her the night before, "I indicated that we needed to speak further and someone would need to come in person to speak with him because I was getting two different stories. That's when basically the conversation ended."

The prosecution played the poor-quality audio from about 2 a.m. that next morning of Sidney telling officers saying he didn't "know why y'all are here" and then confirming, "There is no relationship. There *was* a relationship, and I broke it off," and how Heather called "the other night" and "blew this up." Sidney never said anything about calling Heather from a pay phone.

In cross-examination, Truslow elicited that, according to the police report, Sidney had initially said he had not "seen" her in six weeks, rather than not spoken to her in six weeks. It was a minor point, but one that the defense would build upon as the defense sought to show that in their zeal to nail Sidney, detectives ignored other promising avenues of investigation. Truslow asked about Heather's ex-boyfriend, and Furr said, "I did not develop him as a suspect," though he left open the possibility somebody else at the department had.

"Was that because he was reported to be abusive to Heather?"

"Yes, I was told that. I was not the one that developed him as a suspect."

Exactly who did remained unstated. On redirect questioning, Livesay suggested this was no more than a red herring.

"Did anybody say anything to you about any other man and her being involved in any altercation or anything like that?" she asked.

"No, ma'am."

"If they had of, would you have reached out to that person?"

"I would have."

"Did you reach out to anybody other than the defendant?"

"No, I didn't, no."

"Were you given any information from anybody that night that led you to contact anybody but this defendant?"

"No, I was not."

The most problematic police witness for the prosecution was Peter Cestare, the lieutenant in charge of crime scene sections who was among the officers paying a visit to the Moorer house on Dec. 20, 2013. Cestare would remember seeing security cameras, but said he didn't memorialize this potentially important evidence in any of the 27 photos he took.

No mention of the cameras ever appeared in any police reports either, facts the defense confronted him with, prompting the prosecution to try to bolster Cestare's credibility with corroborating testimony from Jacob Melton, a 17-year-old friend of the Moorers' son.

Mumbling softly through his testimony in a strong South Carolina accent, Jacob told the jury he used to hang out at the Moorers' home

"During that time frame, did you ever see any cameras up at the defendant's house?" asked Livesay.

"Yes, ma'am," he said, recalling the cameras were posted high on the outside of the home overlooking the garage, with the feed going to a monitor in one of the bedrooms. He had seen this as recently as a few weeks before Heather Elvis's disappearance.

Shown a photo taken by Cestare of that same room, Melton said the monitor was no longer there, replaced by a hanging photo.

The defense had ample ammunition to discredit him.

"Nobody's trying to get you into trouble," began Truslow, "but in 2013, were you using marijuana?"

"Yes, sir."

"Are you still using marijuana?"

"No, sir."

The prosecution rebounded with the next witness through which it would introduce the heart of its case. It began with the testimony of Jonathan Lee Martin. Prosecutors introduced the phone records showing the 1:35 a.m. pay phone call to Heather Elvis, her phone's multiple attempts to call that number back, followed by her phone connecting with Sidney's phone for a more than four-minute phone conversation at 3:17 a.m.

"I asked him about phone calls and he indicated there was a phone call from Heather around 2 or 3 in the morning, but she had called him," Martin testified. "I asked him if he had called her at all. He indicated that he had not. I asked him if there were any pay phone calls he had made to her. He indicated that there was not. He actually made a question: Did they still have pay phones? I indicated to him that we were working on getting video from the 10th Avenue pay phone. He then admitted that he had used that pay phone that night and contacted her."

During cross-examination, Martin agreed with Truslow's observation that the records only showed what calls were made when, not who was actually speaking or what was said.

"You don't know who's got (Heather Elvis') phone at that point?"

"No."

"You don't know if she's with anybody during this point in time period?"

"No," said Martin, though he added, "If you go off his statement, though, she talked to him on that phone at some point. Heather talked to Sidney on that phone."

"But you don't know whether she's alone, is what I'm saying?"

"No."

"You don't even know if during the time she's making these calls if she is driving her own vehicle?"

"No."

"Do you know if she's a passenger in her own vehicle?"

"I do not."

"You don't know if she's driving in another vehicle at that time?"

"I do not."

As for the pay phone call, "Did you ask him what was going on?"

"I did."

"What explanation did he give you for making the pay phone call?"

"He said he was trying to reach her to tell her to stop harassing him."

"Did he mention further issues about notes being left on his car?"

"He did mention something along the lines that she had placed some notes on his vehicle."

"Did he mention in this interview with you about that potentially causing trouble with his wife?"

"He did."

From the phone records, the prosecution went to the video evidence. The jury saw the surveillance video of Sidney buying the pregnancy test at the Walmart, followed by the fuzzy video purported to show Sidney emerging from the bushes at the Kangaroo Express gas station making that pay phone call.

Cross-examining the witness who discussed the Kangaroo footage, Detective Brian Wilson, Truslow asked: "Do you know why he would not pull his truck up to the pay phone in the parking lot of the store to use the pay phone?"

"No, I don't."

"Is it possible he could have had somebody in the vehicle with him that he didn't want to know he was making a phone call?"

"It could be possible, yes," said Wilson.

While the prosecution couldn't prove who was in the cars, they could narrow down where one of those cars went. Aaron Edens, an intelligence analyst from the San Mateo County Sheriff's Department in the San Francisco Bay area, specializes in unlocking secrets inside cell phones. He had been hired by the prosecution on March 26, 2015, more than a year after the arrests of the Moorers, showing how much work had still been left to do to build a case.

Traveling to South Carolina the following July 2015 to conduct further measurements on the ground, Edens created a minute-by-minute log of the movement of Heather's cell phone the night she disappeared, based on GPS data, Google information and pings to nearby cell phone towers.

When Sidney called from the pay phone, Heather's phone was in her apartment and remained there as her phone dialed roommate Brianna and called back the pay phone. Heather's phone moved to the northeast corner of the parking lot at Longbeard's Bar and Grill near the Dumpsters. Her phone then moved a short distance down the road to Augusta Plantation Drive at the entrance to a housing complex, before returning to the Longbeard's parking lot for another 13 minutes, from 3:02 a.m. to 3:15 a.m.

Two more calls went out to the pay phone without getting answered, then about a minute later, the phone moved to White River Drive in front of—or in—Heather's apartment house, where the four-minute call went to Sidney's cell phone. The phone remained there for four more minutes, then moved down white River Drive, to Forest Brook Road, then onto Peachtree Road, ending at the boat landing at 3:37 a.m. From there, four more calls went to Sidney's phone from 3:38 a.m. to 3:41 am.

Again, Truslow sought to show the limitations of this evidence.

"You're not testifying about where a person is or where a particular vehicle is?" asked Truslow. "You cannot testify whether or not Heather was in possession of this phone at this time."

"I cannot testify to that."

The prosecution capped the technical portion of its case with the testimony of Grant Fredericks, perhaps the biggest threat to the defense. After rattling off his credentials—FBI instructor, owner of his company in Spokane, Wash., veteran expert witness in trials around the country—Fredericks gave a mini-lesson in analyzing video images of vehicles at night. He explained what criteria he considered, from the shape of the vehicle to the patterns the headlights splash on the pavements, and how he compares test footage of vehicles to the evidentiary footage.

Likening his avocation to other comparative forensic sciences such as the analysis of shoeprints, tire treads, bullet casings, toolmarks and fingerprints, he said he can determine comparisons from video with astonishing accuracy, as he claimed he did in this case with the footage of the vehicle caught on surveillance video heading to and from Peachtree Landing.

In this case, the known vehicle was Sidney's new Ford F-150. The question was how closely, if at all, the vehicle on the security videos matched the F-150.

In an experiment, Fredericks went out at night with six Ford F-150s from 2013 and 2014 with accessories and headlights. Some were red, the others black. He also brought five non-Fords, including two Chevrolet Silverados in black and silver, two black Dodge Rams and a black GMC Denali.

All of the trucks were driven past the cameras at Highway 814 and Mill Pond Road at what appeared to Fredericks to be the exact locations that the surveillance video was seen under the same lighting and weather conditions. Video of each of the vehicles was subjected to the same inspection as the questioned vehicle.

Livesay asked, "And if you don't mind, after that process, tell this jury: Were you able to determine the class and characteristics of the truck on the surveillance footage?"

"Yes."

"And if you don't mind, tell them the class and characteristics of that truck."

"So after doing all the examinations and tests, all the other non-Ford F-150 vehicles were eliminated. They all had significant identifiable differences. Based on that, the only vehicle that could be the questioned vehicle is a Ford F-150 King Cab."

"So it was a black Ford F-150?"

"Yes, Limited Edition."

One of the key identifiers, he said, was the F-150 Limited Edition's high-end HID headlights, which made a distinctive pattern on the roadway.

The prosecution had previously called a manager from Beach Automotive Group of Myrtle Beach to the stand to testify that his dealership sold that very year, make and model of truck, down to the specialized headlamps, to Sidney Moorer, who traded in his old 2010 white F-150.

Fredericks didn't conduct a test on Sidney's truck. By the time he was on the case, somebody had changed the headlights on Sidney's truck, throwing off its most distinctive feature. So Fredericks relied on test video the Horry County Police Department shot from those locations on Feb. 24, 2014, when the truck still had the same headlights.

Based on everything he saw, it was a match, he said.

"Have you ever seen two different vehicles have the same headlight spread pattern?" asked Livesay.

"No," he said, "none are identical, even off the assembly line."

This marked the final major element in the prosecution's case, allegedly putting Sidney's truck on the road, driving to and from Peachtree Landing, at times dovetailing with phone records, at the very moment and location Heather's phone—and perhaps Heather—went dead.

The defense had strongly objected to allowing Fredericks' testimony. At a pretrial hearing two months earlier, in April, Truslow brought in his own witness, a former FBI agent named Bruce Koenig who had headed the department's audio-visual investigative department. Koenig vouched for Frederick's methods and analysis, agreeing that he could determine the surveillance videos showed that year and model of Ford F-150. But he said it was overstatement to say the vehicle in the video was Sidney's F-150. "When you say something is truly unique, you have to be able to say that every other vehicle of that type cannot match these other characteristics," he said.

Judge Dennis overruled the defense objection and allowed Fredericks' testimony, saying he qualified as a courtroom expert and that it would be up to the jury to determine, subject to cross-examination, whether Fredericks was correct.

Truslow had already laid the groundwork for an attack on Fredericks, deriding the security video as nothing but a "black blur" and mocking Fredericks as a hired gun who could present no scientific studies and no research to back up his claims. "This is his baby he cooked up for this case," said Truslow in his opening.

The lawyer began his cross-examination by attacking Fredericks's academic credentials, eliciting that he got his undergraduate degree, not in one of the sciences, but in broadcasting.

"Emphasis in engineering," Fredericks added, to which Truslow noted that Fredericks's curriculum vitae says nothing about such an emphasis. Fredericks simply sat stone-faced and didn't respond.

This set the tone for the cross-examination. While expert witnesses are notoriously prickly about having their credentials and opinions challenged by lawyers, Fredericks displayed the fruits of his 150 courtroom appearances. He betrayed no irritation, never got defensive. When Truslow asked pointedly, "Have you ever published a study on headlight spread pattern analysis?," he answered calmly, "I have not. There are many studies published on it. But I haven't published." He didn't elaborate and didn't try to defend himself.

If anything, as the questioning progressed, it was Truslow who became flustered, at one point stumbling through questions packed with the words such as "differences of the headlight spread pattern" and "dirt on composite lenses," until Fredericks deadpanned, "I'm not sure I understand your question."

Going back to what his own expert had said during the pretrial hearing, Truslow tried to show a basic flaw in Fredericks's comparison between the truck in the surveillance video and Sidney's truck in the police test video. Truslow noted that the test video was taken months after Heather's disappearance.

"You are aware that during those two months that my client continued to use his vehicle day in, day out in ordinary life?"

"I don't know how long he had the vehicle before police seized it."

"Driving that truck for two months, hitting bumps, floods, everything else, would that make a difference to you?"

"No," Fredericks said. "The patterns shift over time for various reasons. In this case, there weren't."

Truslow then sought to show that Fredericks has had his credibility challenged before in another case.

"Did you have some problems in that case with your testimony?"

"I didn't testify in that case," he corrected.

"Your report?"

"No, I had no problems with that."

The case involved a boy killed while riding his bicycle. It was first thought he was killed when he was hit by a car driven by an off-duty police officer. Fredericks had come to the conclusion that the boy actually lost control of his bike and wasn't hit by the officer's vehicle.

"Did you learn thereafter that the young boy's DNA was found on the bumper of the vehicle?"

That was incorrect, Fredericks said, calling it "transfer DNA" from people at the scene who transferred it to the bumper by mistake.

This one fizzling, Truslow moved on to another case. It involved a mentally disabled man who died after a confrontation with a police officer wielding a baton. Truslow suggested that Fredericks had been caught coming to the wrong conclusion in the case.

Fredericks said that wasn't true, either.

"My client fabricated evidence and put my name on it," he said. When he found out, he hired his own attorney and went to a federal judge. "The judge evaluated all my comments and he agreed and wrote a finding that the U.S. federal attorney withheld evidence from the defense. That's where the case is."

Truslow took issue with Fredericks's portrayal of the case. The prosecution then objected that the line of questioning had veered too far from the Sidney Moorer case.

"It goes to credibility," Truslow told the judge.

"I'm ruling that you move on to something else," the judge said.

Only the defense had nowhere to move.

"I have nothing further," said Truslow.

The prosecution didn't question Fredericks further. It wasn't so much a defeat for the defense as an opportunity lost.

After reaching a peak of influence with shows such as "CSI," where complicated cases can be solved with the miracle of science, forensic evidence has in recent years begun to lose its luster with juries and come under successful attack by defense attorneys. (Truslow declined to comment for this book.)

With the defense on its heels, the prosecution unloaded its most emotionally powerful evidence, introducing the angry text conversation between Heather Elvis and somebody— Sidney or Tammy or both.

Projected on a big screen in the courtroom, the jury read along with investigator Will Lynch the string of messages that included, "Somebody's about to get their ass beat down. You, bitch, is about to take her last breath," "Hey sweetie you ready to meet the Mrs.," and "Your skank ass needs to leave me alone. Stop stalking me you crazy fucking whore."

During cross, Truslow could only ask: "Do you know whether those text messages came from Sidney or from Tammy?"

Lynch said, "All I know is what phone they came from." Sidney's phone.

The prosecution wrapped up its case by calling Brianna Warrelmann. The former friend, roommate and confidante of Heather Elvis, who used to party with her and work with her at the Tilted Kilt, was now a poised young woman, recently married with a 10-month-old son and a stepdaughter. Like Stephen Schiraldi, her presence suggested the future that Heather never had.

She began by recounting the relationship between Heather and Sidney, the night after the baseball game, Heather and Sidney on the patio, talking past closing time.

"How long did this relationship go on as far as the two of them?" asked Livesay.

"All summer."

Brianna portrayed the relationship as more meaningful than a mere fling. "You could tell that both of them cared about each other," she said, remembering the coffee and snacks Sidney brought Heather.

"Do you know if that relationship ever developed into a sexual relationship?"

"I do. It did."

"At some point, did that relationship end?"

"It did, when Sidney's wife found out."

"What started going on once the relationship ended?"

"Harassing phone calls, text messages, photos were sent to Heather."

"What kind of photos?"

"Sexual photos of Sidney and Tammy."

"During the time that Heather and Sidney were together, was she with anybody else?"

"No, not during the time they were together."

"Did any other men come and see her?"

"Friends would come and see her at the Tilted Kilt, but her heart was completely invested in Sidney."

"Did you ever notice any physical changes in her during that time?"

"Yes, I want to say it would be the end of September, beginning of October 2013, she had put on some weight. I actually know that because she went up a full cup size. When you work at Tilted Kilt, you have to have a special bra for your shirt, and she had to get a new bra for work and had to get new bras in general."

"At that time, what did she think was going on?"

"She thought she was pregnant."

Echoing the testimony of Heather's coworkers, Brianna said Heather returned to her normal self by the beginning of December. "She was doing really, really well. You know, us and a bunch of the girls from Tilted Kilt, we would all hang out. We would have a girls night. We'd talk for hours and hours all night long about life and our goals and hopes."

Brianna said she was with Heather most hours outside of work. When they weren't together, they were texting each other.

"During that time, did y'all ever ride by to Sidney Moorer's house?"

"No."

"During that time did y'all ever leave any notes on his vehicle?"

"No."

Brianna said she knew nothing about Sidney buying a black Ford F-150. The only truck she'd seen him drive was the white pickup.

The last time Brianna saw Heather was that Monday morning in December when Brianna left early to go to New Jersey for Christmas break.

"She was sleeping on my couch, and then she woke up just as I was about to leave and begged me not to go because she said she was going to miss her other half."

They spoke on the phone, texted and Snapchatted while Brianna was gone, with Heather telling her how excited she was about getting the makeup artist job.

"And if you don't mind, tell this jury about the last time that you talked to her."

"At 1:44 a.m., she called me crying," Brianna said, her voice breaking up. "Not like sobbing, but hysterically crying. And when I asked her what was wrong, she didn't want to tell me because she knew that I didn't approve of her relationship with Sidney in the slightest bit. She said nothing was wrong. I told her she was lying. She told me Sidney called."

Through a wavering voice, Brianna recounted how Heather only answered because she didn't recognize the local 843 number on her phone, that Sidney said he missed her and had left his wife and wanted to see her. Brianna changed the subject and Heather's mood lifted as she spoke about her date earlier that evening with Stephen Schiraldi.

"She said that she learned how to drive a stick shift," said Brianna. She put her hand to her face, crying softly. Livesay put a cup of water in front of her. Brianna sniffled and said, "She knew that would make me proud."

Brianna took in a heavy breath and recalled how Heather said she planned to meet Stephen later that day. Brianna then brought up the subject of Sidney again, and whether Heather planned to see him. "She told me she was going to sleep on it and not make any rash decisions and that she would talk to me in the morning and that she loved me," said Brianna. "And that was the end of the conversation. That was the last time I heard from her."

Livesay asked, "Was she afraid of Tammy Moorer?"

"Yes, ma'am."

"Was she afraid of Sidney?"

"I don't believe so."

After the emotionally heated testimony, a chilly reception awaited Truslow for cross-examination.

"Good morning, Miss Warrelmann."

Brianna didn't reply.

"It's your understanding that we're here today for the trial of Sidney Moorer?"

"Yes, sir."

"And not Tammy Moorer?"

"I'm well aware."

"Heather was afraid of Tammy Moorer and not afraid of Sidney?"

"Correct."

"You believe that Sidney and Heather cared about each other?"

"I did."

Truslow then made a rare venture into the matter of Heather's pregnancy concerns. He asked her if Heather could not have been pregnant since she had had her period. "She did spot before I left for winter break," she said. She had found her tampons. "I'm the one who usually cleaned the bedroom."

Truslow showed Brianna her statement to police in which she said, "She then got her period."

On the stand, Brianna would only go so far as to say, "She did bleed."

Truslow then asked about Heather's abusive ex-boyfriend. Brianna said that Heather forgave him and they got along well enough that she lived with him briefly.

"He kicked her out?"

"He did. He was having his ex-girlfriend come to live with him because they wanted to work on their relationship and he didn't believe that Heather should still be staying there when the ex-girlfriend moved in."

He also asked about Heather's problems at home. She described Heather as "the rebellious child" who didn't see eye-to-eye sometimes with her parents and sometimes put them through hell, just as Brianna had done with her parents in those days.

Truslow asked her about young men Heather knew. Out of the blue, he asked, "Do you know whether or not either of those individuals are registered sex offenders?"

"I do not."

Livesay got up. "Your honor, at this point I have to object. I have no idea where this is going. Is it relevant?"

The judge overruled her objection, but after showing Brianna a photograph and asking if she recognized the person, Livesay objected again, and the line of inquiry— along with the rest of cross-examination—ended.

After a couple of mop-up questions from the prosecution, the judge asked Livesay, "Do you have another witness?"

"At this time," she said, "the state rests."

The defense called no witnesses. The trial went to closing arguments.

18.

"We are here because Heather Elvis, a 20-year-old young woman, is not here," Nancy Livesay began. "Sometimes we forget, because we see the defendant every day. You see me every day. So we forget the reason we're here is because there's somebody else who isn't here. Don't forget that."

On June 23, 2016, the prosecution tried to ride the momentum from Brianna's testimony, the weak attack on the video evidence, the profane punch of those text messages, the phone records and Sidney's initial lie to police about not calling Heather from the pay phone.

But despite all that evidence, Livesay asserted, "This is not only Sidney Moorer's day. This is Heather Elvis's day.

"The question is: Why isn't she here? What happened to this 20-year-old young woman? I'm here to tell you that that woman was kidnapped. She did not vanish voluntarily. This is a woman who was taken way too early. This is a woman who has not even lived life yet. This is a woman who had not even begun to have life experiences. You are talking about a 20-year-old woman who has never been married, never had kids, never owned her own home."

Livesay acknowledged what could be the major hurdle for the jury, the lack of direct evidence. She tried to turn that into a positive. "This case has better evidence than if we had an eyewitness," she said. "If we had an eyewitness up here, everyone would be wondering: Is that what they really saw in the dark? Is this person biased? Are they confused? Can they remember what they saw at 3:30 in the morning? Then it would be a credibility issue. We don't have any credibility issues in this case. All we have is hard facts, records and data."

This case, she said, "is a circumstantial case, but this is the best evidence anybody could ask for." Livesay then ran through the evidence and testimony again, from Heather's relationship with Sidney, through the breakup, the nasty text exchange, the pay phone call, the phone records showing Heather's final hours, the surveillance footage she argued showed Sidney's truck, to the last phone activity from her phone out at Peachtree Landing.

"The snag with this case was the pregnancy," Livesay said. Heather suspected she was pregnant and that Sidney found out about it. That's why Sidney bought a pregnancy test at Walmart, then right after that called Heather. "When a 40-year-old man is calling a 20-year-old girl in the middle of the night from a pay phone, something bad is about to happen. There are some bad intentions there," Livesay. "He's sneaking around calling from pay phones and then lying about it to the police. So you know he is up to no good."

Only Heather didn't know that. "She was mad at him. She was trying to move on with her life. For some reason— even I'd do it—as mad as you get, in five minutes you have convinced yourself that, 'He wants to be with me, and that he loves me and that it's me he's thinking about.' And before you knew it, she had it roped around in her mind that 'I'm going to meet him.' At the time I'm sure, she didn't realize the danger in it."

So she went to Peachtree Landing. "This has got to be one of darkest holes in Horry County," Livesay said. "There's one way in, one way out." Sidney now has "a little girl, 20 years old, down there at a landing in the middle of the night with nobody else around."

And Heather only called one person. "She's calling Sidney Moore. I'm sure she's like: 'Where are you? It's dark as hell out here.' See, she didn't suspect trouble. She expected a familiar face. She was excited. She was calling him earlier ready to see him. She doesn't know danger is amongst her. She doesn't know she's being led down a dark hole."

By the time the first cop rolled up at 4 a.m., "that woman has already been taken. There's not one broken glass, no sign of struggle. She had her keys and her license in the car," said Livesay. "She had no idea this person she was excited to see had evil intentions. It was never a fair matchup. She was 20, no life experience, and she was tangling with a 40-year-old man who had a lot of life experiences."

And make no mistake, Livesay said, Sidney was the only man at issue. Livesay called it "so disturbing" for the defense to mention the names of other men, men who Heather didn't call that night and with whom she had not had a relationship recently. "There is not one shred of evidence that points to anybody else. Nobody else knew where that woman was but the same man that she had been trying to get in touch with and talking to all night long. (It's) Sidney Moorer."

If anything, Heather's troubles with her family played into Sidney's hand. "She slept in her car a few nights, a rebel doing her own thing," she said. "Wouldn't that make for an easy victim? A woman that you know doesn't get along with her family. He thought no one's even going to miss this woman."

Until now, it was a solid summation. But it began to go off the rails. Livesay repeated herself.

As she spoke more about the pay phone call, more about the surveillance footage, more about Heather's possible pregnancy, more about how Heather had to have been kidnapped by somebody she trusted, until finally the judge interrupted her. "You've been arguing for over an hour. It's been somewhat repetitive at some points."

Abruptly, Livesay wrapped up. "I'm going to ask you to find him guilty of kidnapping. Everything points to him. And that woman is no longer around. Thank you for your time."

It was a bumpy landing to an otherwise soaring closing, and it gave the defense extra hope going into Truslow's arguments. "This case is about Heather Elvis. It is a tragedy," the attorney began. "But the trial today is about the fate of Sidney Moorer."

With such high stakes, he said, the circumstantial evidence as presented by the prosecution didn't measure up. "Any prosecutor, anywhere, in any case wants to have direct evidence. They want to have eyewitnesses, confessions, forensic evidence, fingerprints, DNA. They don't want to be left with a circumstantial case because it's hard to convict on that. The reason it's hard is because there's a fine line between circumstantial evidence and looking suspicious."

That's why he mentioned those other men. "The only thing I know is that Sidney Moorer did not kidnap Heather Elvis. I do not know what happened. I cannot prove he didn't kidnap Heather Elvis. I cannot prove that somebody else did not do something, because you can't prove a negative. Therefore, it's on the state to prove every circumstance beyond a reasonable doubt."

The questions about the men, he explained, "was to demonstrate to you the ease with which suspicion and unfortunate circumstances can make you look bad or point the direction at you." Law enforcement should have explored these men further, he said.

"What happened was that they had a lot of pressure to do something because this case, unlike other cases, immediately garnered big-time media coverage, immediately," he said. "And within a day, Sidney Moorer's name is out there, because Heather Elvis's father had called him. He had heard she had dated him. Then the social media starts and the names Sidney Moorer and Tammy Moorer are all over it."

After only two months of investigation, police arrested the Moorers, leaving prosecutors with more than two years to build a case. "They focused on one person to the exclusion of anybody else. The inherent danger in that is you have to find stuff on this guy, you have to make it look bad, you have to make him look bad."

But that, he said, wasn't evidence. "The amount of suspicious things that they give you does not make it substantial circumstantial evidence. It is the weight of the circumstantial evidence, or the pieces of circumstantial evidence, that you find beyond a reasonable doubt that you then analyze."

When the jury really examines the evidence, it would find it lacking, he said. Truslow argued that everything that looked bad could be explained away. Sidney was driving around at night because those were the hours he kept as a graveyard shift maintenance man when restaurants were closed; police had no photos of the security cameras at Sidney's house because they didn't exist. "That's just baloney," he said of the officer's testimony, and marijuana-smoking Jacob Melton's testimony couldn't change that.

Sidney had to use the pay phone because his wife had the cell phone and Sidney didn't want Tammy to know what he was talking to Heather about. "Let's say that he called and told her what Heather Elvis told Brianna he said. For the sake of argument," said Truslow, "not one witness from the ladies from the Tilted Kilt all the way through have even given you any piece of evidence that Sidney Moorer, in any way, was mean or untoward to Heather, was anything but caring. Maybe he did want to leave his wife and be with her."

If so, then that would not explain why Sidney would kidnap her. "Serious felony cases more likely than not come from seeing red," he said. "They come from a passion, and I don't mean a good passion, but a rage and a passion. Sidney displayed that at no time. Nobody has testified or shown any time in his life where he has been an angry or passionate or mean person, in general, or towards Heather."

Tammy Moorer, on the other hand, had plenty of reason to be angry at Heather, an anger expressed in that text exchange. "That is a point in time where it's undisputed, if you look at it, that Tammy Moorer is on the iPhone with Heather Elvis and even pretending to be Sidney Moorer. Why do I say that's important? That night on Dec. 18, he doesn't have a cell phone. He has to use a pay phone. All the other stuff that they say lures her to Peachtree Landing comes from the iPhone."

That Truslow would add Tammy to the list of people who may have wished harm on Heather was a startling suggestion, and certainly one that could cause problems for Sidney with her. She had allegedly cuffed him to bed for less. But Truslow double-downed.

Maybe, Truslow said, Tammy lured Heather to the landing. Maybe, he said, Tammy said, "Let's meet at the landing. Sidney's an asshole. He's been with you and with me."

Truslow said, "If you believe that was the same F-150, ask yourself, who was driving it? Who has motive to want to do something like this? Is it the person who has not shown any kind of aggressive behavior or mean behavior to anybody, including Heather Elvis, other than bringing her Starbucks coffee and calling her saying, I still want to be with you?

"Or is it the person that the first three witnesses said that even after the relationship was found out and stopped, continued to harass and threaten and would not let it go with Heather Elvis, even to the point of sending pornographic photos of her and her husband to Heather Elvis?

"That shows you a state of mind. That shows you something in your mind that will not go away. Those kind of things feed on themselves. That anger feeds on itself and it doesn't go away. If Tammy Moorer wants to drive the F-150, Tammy Moorer is driving the F-150."

That is *if* the truck ever got there. He urged the jury to reject the video evidence. "I don't believe that stuff. I don't," he said. "I tried to make that clear to you. Basically, what Mr. Fredericks is telling you is that no two vehicles anywhere have the same headlight (spread). It's not based on science, nor is he a scientist."

In the end, Truslow said, "I am not prosecuting Tammy Moorer. I am defending Sidney Moorer. Tammy Moorer is charged with kidnapping. Tammy Moorer's trial is coming up. It will be in this courtroom. There will be 12 other people who will decide what happens. I'm merely asking you to use your common sense and you come up with the more likely scenario, because if you don't, somebody's getting convicted for something they didn't do."

Truslow looked at Sidney. "I'm sure that my client doesn't like everything that I'm saying. But I have to go where the facts lead me. I'm sure he doesn't want to think that about his wife. I'm not sure if it's crossed his mind. It is his wife, or more importantly the mother of his three children. I'm not even sure I want to sit next to him when I go over there. But I'll tell you this. I'm going to say what I have to say as I see it."

19.

Getting a dozen people to agree on anything is hard enough. A dozen people would struggle to form a consensus on lunch. Getting them to agree on something so serious that it could send a man to prison can strain even the most decisive individual. Defense attorneys rely on that. They just need one.

Whether Kirk Truslow really did go rogue on Sidney and throw Tammy Moorer under the bus wasn't known. It's hard to imagine a defense attorney making such a major tactical decision without clearing it first with his client. Either way, it might have worked.

After final instructions in the law by Judge R. Markley Dennis Jr., the case went to the jury at about 4:45 p.m. Thursday. The panel broke for evening about 7:20 p.m. and returned at 9 a.m. Friday. They reviewed pieces of evidence, including the tape of Sidney's interview in his driveway, and asked for the definitions of circumstantial evidence, reasonable doubt and to hear the charge of kidnapping.

At 2:40 p.m., after less than a full day of deliberations, the jury sent a note to the judge. It was deadlocked and wanted to know what to do.

The law allows for a process at this point, one most defense attorneys dislike. They are given what's called the Allen Charge, also called the "hammer charge" or "dynamite charge," designed to shake up things in the jury room and get them talking in new ways.

The instruction takes the form of a long lecture by the judge. Jurors were brought into the courtroom, and Judge Dennis told them: "It's normal for jurors to disagree at first. But the fact that we normally get a verdict also means that after reasonable persons lay aside all extraneous matters and determine to decide a case on the basis of the law and the evidence, then they do come to a common understanding and a verdict."

Since this jury couldn't do that yet, he offered some suggestions. "It may help to tell other jurors how you feel about the case. I'm sure you've already done that to a large extent, and I'm not suggesting that you haven't. On the other hand, it may help if other jurors exchange views with you, and I ask that you listen to each other. And I'm sure that you've done that. But I'm going to ask you to revisit that again, and to give deference to each side, and to be willing to compare and consider what one is saying that may disagree with your respective decision."

The judge made it clear what the consequences of a lack of agreement were. "I say that for this reason: a mistrial is a very unfortunate thing. If you as jurors cannot agree on a verdict, it doesn't mean that anybody wins and the case is over. It simply means that at some future time, that another jury will sit where you are, and a trial with the same participants will come in, the same lawyers will likely appear, the same questions will be asked and will presumably get the same answers. So we'll go through this entire process again."

While the next jury may be no more able to come to a decision can't be known, he said, but the implication is clear. Try a little harder so we don't have to do this all over again.

"I want you to go back in to the jury room, again telling other jurors the weakness of your position and listening to the strengths of theirs. You should not interrupt each other or comment on each other other's views until one has had a full chance to talk. During this process, the course of your deliberations, each of you should not hesitate to reexamine your own views and to change your opinion if you're convinced if it's erroneous."

The judge sent the jury back into the deliberation room to give it one more go.

Another note came to the judge.

"The jury is still deadlocked," the judge told the courtroom, "and will be unable to resolve it. The jury has received instructions, they're still deadlocked."

This left him no choice. "I'll declare a mistrial and this case will be tried again."

The judge thanked the spectators "for the decorum that has been demonstrated and displayed" and asked "that everyone continue to maintain that same proper decorum and respect for the process." To the bailiff, he said, "Bring in the jury, please."

He informed the jury that a mistrial had been declared and thanked them for their service. "I appreciate your diligence and your conscientious attempt to resolve this dispute. No one is expected to give up their sincere conscientious feelings, and that's why this system works as well as it does."

With the gag order in place, people had to parse their reactions to the mistrial. Debbi Elvis, Heather Elvis's mother, said it was like reliving a nightmare. Kirk Truslow told reporters the outcome was a "little disappointing," but in truth, he was in a good position.

As expected, Solicitor Jimmy Richardson announced his office would try Sidney again on the kidnapping charge. But now, the defense had seen everything the prosecution had to offer. It could learn from its missteps. For the next trial, Truslow said, he had a highly qualified scientist ready to come to court to challenge Grant Fredericks's conclusions.

Only one of the 12 jurors commented to the media, the foreman Fred Lang. "If we were not doing a trial on circumstantial evidence, it would have been a much better way for us to sink our teeth into and come up with a proper verdict," he said. "But because of the fact there were so many what-ifs, 'what if this happened,' 'what if that happened,' and things of that nature, we were hopelessly deadlocked. Even though the state was saying that there was a possibility of him being there, of him doing this, there was no concrete evidence of the fact it happened. We were questioning in our own mind: It could have been somebody else? We didn't do the what ifs."

The jury's final vote: 10 for guilty, two not guilty.

Sidney escaped by the skin of his teeth. But he still escaped. He was a free man. From the very beginning, his lawyers had relied on the power of "what if." This had helped get Sidney out on bond. It helped convinced a judge to let him move out of the state. It probably played into the prosecution's decision to drop the murder charge.

But whatever relief he may have felt was short lived.

On the second day of his kidnapping trial, a matter came and went so quickly it barely registered. It seemed the prosecution's suggestion Sidney had bought the Walmart pregnancy test for Heather left him fuming. He was so mad he called a local television station, WBTW, to set the record straight.

"I was actually buying it for my wife," he told the station. "She was in the vehicle when I bought it for her. She took it that night, and it was negative, like so many before and after."

Asked why he thought the prosecutor introduced it, he said, "I know the prosecution's desperate. They need a conviction really, really bad, but I think what they need more than that is that they need the truth. They need to give the family peace, real peace, what really, really happened."

The interview was recorded and aired during the trial, which was brought to the judge's attention. He was livid. Judge Dennis interrupted testimony about the surveillance video of the truck to confront Sidney: "You understand the gag order still follows, sir?"

"Um, yes, sir," Sidney said.

"And that is absolutely contrary to the gag order? It violates the gag order, no question about it."

At the time, the judge told Livesay, "I don't know that I have the need to have a contempt proceeding. At some point in time, we'll address that and I'll defer a conclusion."

That point arrived a little over a month after the mistrial. On July 29, 2016, the judge held a contempt hearing. Truslow told the judge that Moorer realized that calling the reporter was a "tremendous blunder."

Sidney himself apologized. "I probably shouldn't have said anything," he said.

The judge was not assuaged. "You had every right to say what you wanted to say and protect your wife, but you had to do it in this process and what you did has perverted the process because you put out what was said and nobody had the right to challenge."

He then sentenced Sidney to five months in jail for contempt of court. Sidney emptied his pockets and was led out of the courtroom. Sidney served 61 days, let out early for time he'd already spent in jail and for good behavior. As he left J. Reuben Long Detention Center, reporters greeted him with questions, most of which he answered with a terse, "I'm not going to talk about that."

But when asked if he had a message for Heather Elvis's family, he said, "They should demand the truth, not somebody going to jail. They should demand the truth, period."

It was, perhaps, an ill-advised comment from somebody who had already spent two months in jail for running off his mouth. Sidney suffered no judicial reprisals this time, his remarks sneaking just inside the acceptable boundaries of the gag order. He was about to have more good luck.

For the retrial on the kidnapping charge, his lawyers sought a change of venue. "There is no way in hell I will ever get a fair trial in Horry County," Sidney once complained to the *Sun News*. The court reviewed hundreds questionnaires sent to prospective jurors. Sure enough, it found that the county had been so "saturated" with social media posts about the case that even those juror prospects stating they could be unbiased and impartial were at risk of taint. The court received "a number of reports" of potential jurors saying on Facebook they "know how to get around the Judge by just saying that they can be unbiased," according to court documents.

At the defense request, the kidnapping retrial would be moved from Horry County down the coast to Georgetown County. Sidney's camp had reason to rejoice in knowing they'd get a second shot at the kidnapping case with potentially friendlier (or at least less hostile) jurors.

It was another legal victory, putting Sidney a step closer to his often-stated goal of total exoneration. He had every reason for confidence moving on to his next trial—that separate trial he had requested on the obstruction of justice charge. The stakes were lower, a maximum 10-year term instead of the 30 for kidnapping, and the evidence and witnesses would be mostly the same.

Sidney had one more thing in his favor. The Horry County Police Department had plunged into scandal. One of the officers under siege was involved in the Heather Elvis case.

20.

One new face, one familiar sat at the prosecution table. Nancy Livesay was back for the Solicitor's Office, joined for this trial by Josh Holford, an assistant solicitor, tasked with delivering the opening statement. The issue before the jury wasn't whether Sidney had abducted Heather, it was whether he impeded the investigation into whoever did, even if it were Sidney.

"Heather Elvis is still missing," Holford told the jury of 11 men and one woman. "Could that have changed had the defendant not obstructed the investigation? Could law enforcement have run down the proper leads, realized that this was a little more suspicious than they thought it was in the beginning?"

Defense attorney James Galmore made his debut in the case by focusing his opening statement on the law, not the evidence, stressing that the prosecution has to prove guilt beyond a reasonable doubt. "You have to be firmly convinced of the guilt of the accused," said Galmore, tapping the edge of the jury box to punctuate his point. "You're here to judge the case based on what evidence comes from that witness stand and that alone."

Much of the case would turn on how the jury reacted to Sidney's statements to police. So the prosecution again called Cpl. Danny Furr to recount that first phone to Sidney in which Sidney claimed that Heather had called him instead of the other way around.

"If you had known about the pay phone call or that he talked to her twice after midnight, would you have done anything different?" asked Holford.

"It would have ended up being a suspicious missing person," he said, bringing additional detectives on board. As he had at the kidnapping trial, he acknowledged under cross-examination he didn't make a report about his phone call with Sidney, nor did he record the call, but he did send patrol officers to talk to Sidney, and the scratchy audio of that driveway conversation also was played as it had been before.

Detective Jonathan Martin returned to court and again recounted the speedy work getting Heather's phone records showing that she had received a pay phone call and her many attempts to reach Sidney's cell phone after that, finally connecting with him.

"Did his story match up with the phone records that you'd received?" asked Holford.

"His initial statements, no."

During cross-examination, Martin said that once Sidney had been confronted with the pay phone call, he told the truth about reaching out to Heather.

"How much time had lapsed in between that?" Truslow asked.

"Ten, 15 seconds," Martin said.

"Ten or 15 seconds? How were you impeded in 10 seconds by that, or obstructed?"

"It's still a lie," Martin said.

"I know, and it's bad to lie, but he's charged with a crime called obstruction of justice," Truslow said, suggesting that criminal investigations often encounter people who lie.

"Does it all come out cleanly?"

"When people aren't hiding something," Martin said. "Usually."

If the prosecution had its way, the jury would be able decide for itself. For this trial, rather than having Martin paraphrase the police station interview with Sidney, the prosecution wanted to roll out the entire audiotape of the session. The defense wanted the judge to bar the interview tape from the obstruction trial.

At a pretrial hearing, the defense argued that Sidney had never been read his Miranda rights, that famous recitation from countless cop shows telling a perp they have the right to remain silent, that anything they say can and will be used against them in court, that they have the right to an attorney, and if they can't afford counsel a lawyer will appointed.

TV and the movies give the impression these rights are read immediately. In fact, the law only requires the reading of Miranda when somebody is under arrest, in a so-called custodial situation. If they're merely being questioned, they're on their own. There's some gray area surrounding the definition of custodial. Being shut up in a room crowded by two detectives, as Sidney was, may strike many as tantamount to being in custody.

But in this situation, Sidney claimed, police took it farther when Sgt. Allen Large, one of the detectives on the case, supposedly cussed out Sidney, threw him against a wall and told him he couldn't leave until he cooperated. Although Tammy did go, Sidney stayed behind and talked to detectives Martin and Cauble.

At a July 31, 2017, hearing, the defense requested that the interview with Martin and Cauble be suppressed, while the prosecution argued it was admissible on the grounds that Sidney gave it voluntarily and was never in custody. The hearing received heavy media coverage because the interview was played for the first time publicly. But the headlines focused on the handcuffing and pay phone lie and not the nuances of Miranda. With little fanfare, the judge allowed the interview into evidence.

So for more than 40 minutes, Sidney's voice and those of detectives Martin and Jeff Cauble filled the courtroom, as Sidney could be heard denying his pay phone call to

Heather until confronted with the ruse that police had him on security video, as well as the talk of sex in the parking lot, the dash into Walmart for the pregnancy test, the notes he said Heather left him on his truck, and the salacious details about Tammy cuffing him to the bed.

Afterward, Cauble, who had since retired from the department and now worked as a manager at a gym, was asked by Livesay to sum up the interview. "We were able to distinguish through phone records that he was telling us the truth about certain things, but that he was leaving things out as well," he said.

As obstruction, it hardly ranked with Watergate, but Cauble and other police witnesses kept insisting that had Sidney been more forthcoming, it would have saved time, streamlined the investigation, maybe even led to the discovery of Heather, all of which seemed like a stretch. The real impact of the interview was the jury's chance to pick up on the subtleties lost in a retelling, Sidney's dodging and weaving, his convenient memory lapses, his seeming lack of concern for a woman he until very recently had a steamy romance with, his utter passiveness, bordering on submissiveness, in the face of his wife.

Stuck with the tape, Truslow took a two-pronged approach in cross-examination.

"How many interviews did Mr. Moorer give that day? Separate interviews?"

"Probably two."

"Did he have one with him and his wife at the same time?"

"I believe so, yes. I was not part of that."

"When he voluntarily came down there, who was the investigator that he said he sat with before any interviews?"

"It was Detective Large."

"Detective Allen Large?"

"Yes."

This was prong one. Bring up Allen Large as many times as possible.

This even though Allen Large was not on the witness list, his work never to be mentioned by the prosecution, the tape of his interviews with Sidney and Tammy never to reach jurors' ears. The reason Truslow couldn't say Large's name enough was because the detective was now a pariah in South Carolina law enforcement.

Floating over the obstruction trial like a noxious cloud was the turmoil facing the Horry County Police Department, much of it due to Sgt. Allen Large.

A 25-plus year veteran of the department, Large encountered serious problems in another case, one that began on May 21, 2015, long after he started work in the Elvis disappearance. The first sign of trouble came on July 4, 2015, when Large was hit with a sexual harassment complaint.

An internal investigation was launched, and on July 31, he got this letter from Chief Saundra Rhodes: "An internal investigation and phone records have sustained these allegations. Due to the findings of this investigation, it is necessary to terminate your employment with the Horry County Police Department, effective immediately."

None of this was known at the time, due to employee confidentiality rules and the gag order in Heather's case. Only months later did reporters discover that Large was the unidentified detective named in a civil lawsuit filed against the department by a woman using the Jane Doe pseudonym.

According to the suit, as Large investigated a report of sexual assault against this Jane Doe, he insisted on meeting her at her home, and then himself assaulted her.

"Over the course of the next six months, Detective engaged in a course of coercive behavior, unwanted sexual advances, and sexual assault," the suit alleges. "On at least one occasion, the Plaintiff was sexually assaulted by Detective within a police vehicle issued by the Horry County Police Department."

Fearful of retribution, the woman didn't initially report Large. Once she filed the lawsuit, the floodgates opened. Four more women would come forward with similar sexual assault allegations against him.

The Horry County Police Department was in full crisis mode.

The more details that emerged, the more tawdry and headline-worthy the scandal became. One of the alleged victims would claim that Large forced her to participate in "catfights" with other women in which they ripped off each other's clothes. Large allegedly made videos of the fights, at least one of which took place in his house.

Large proved to be his own worst enemy. In a deposition obtained by the *Sun News*, Large admitted to staging the fights, but said the women were paid. He justified it by saying that two of the women "were already engaged in doing stuff that was definitely illegal and hardly getting anything for it."

Court papers suggested that at least one other officer was present during the catfighting. By early 2016, Chief Rhodes had asked state officials to investigate three more of her officers, including one who had resigned. A grand jury returned five indictments against Large alleging criminal sexual misconduct. He was offered a plea deal and rejected it, preferring to take his chances at trial.

In April 2016, Rhodes, too, was gone. She pulled the pin, taking retirement after 23 years with the department.

Then about two weeks before the obstruction of justice trial, news outlets reported that the department's deputy chief of police, Maurice Jones, had not, in fact, taken a normal retirement after 33 years of service as originally reported, but resigned after an internal investigation found instances of misconduct and dishonesty. Jones allegedly ordered a police employee to administratively drop, without investigation, 53 open cases, including those belonging to Large and two others linked to the sexual assault allegations.

With this incendiary information swirling around, Large was not called to testify in Sidney's obstruction trial and many others in which he was a key investigator. This prevented what surely would have been a blistering cross-examination, shifting attention from Sidney Moorer to an attack on the entire Horry County Police Department, but the stench of the crisis lingered.

Though none of the officers who testified had been connected to the catfighting allegations, in this context, everything they said on the witness stand—every denial, every memory lapse, every acknowledgement of doing anything other than absolutely perfect police work—was at risk of greater scrutiny.

Truslow asked Cauble more about Large's interviews with Sidney and Tammy.

"How long did they sit?" Truslow asked.

"I'm not sure. I can't answer that, honestly."

"You have no idea how long it could have been?"

"I'm not sure at this time."

"Do you have any idea what the substance of their conversation was? Was that ever reported back to you in any form?"

"I listened to it, yes, sir, but it's been awhile since I listened to that interview. I listened to that interview after the fact."

"With Large?"

It was one "Large" too many. Livesay had had enough.

"I have to object," she said. "Anything that Mr. Cauble would say outside of his knowledge would be hearsay."

"Overruled," said the judge.

Truslow continued, "Did you listen to an interview between Detective Large and my client?"

"Yes."

"It was recorded?"

"Yes, sir."

"Was Detective Large sitting in the room during your interview?"

"To be totally honest with you, I cannot remember if he was or not."

The defense cross-examination spilled into the next day with Truslow moving to prong two of his attack: pressing Cauble on how just how badly the investigation was harmed by Sidney's momentarily lying.

"Would you agree that in some cases in your job that's your problem?"

"I'm sorry?" he said, appearing taken aback.

"That's your problem, not his, right? I mean, it would be nice to have everything, right? But you don't have everything, right?"

"Right."

"He's under no obligation to tell you his life story, is he?"

"No, he's under no obligation. But why would he hold that information from us?"

Asked what information Sidney didn't provide, Cauble said he misled them by claiming he didn't know where Heather lived, among other details.

"Why do you say he misled you?"

Cauble brought his cop face out of retirement: "If somebody spits in my coffee, I'm not going to try to drink around it. I'm going to assume that all the coffee is contaminated. So I'm going to throw that coffee away and I'm gonna get me a new cup of coffee. In this case, if someone lies to us, and in an investigation, we're assuming that everything else is a lie as well until we figure out if it is the truth or not. Do I think he knew where she was living at the time? Yes, I do think he knew where she was living at the time."

"That's your job to solve this case?"

"Yes, sir."

"What you believe is your opinion or belief? What the jury might believe might be different?"

"Yes, sir."

"What I might believe might be different?"

"Yes, sir."

"So do you have any evidence that he knew where she lived when he made that statement?"

"No, I do not," said Cauble.

"Did you expect him to tell you how many times he went to the bathroom that night? Did you expect him to tell you from 9, 9:30 to 4 in the morning every single thing he did?"

"Yes, sir."

"Why didn't you ask him to do that?"

"I thought," Cauble said, "we were."

As the rest of the trial became a rerun of the kidnapping trial, the prosecution hit an unexpected snag. It came at the least likely of times, when Brianna Warrelmann took the stand recounting her final conversation with Heather.

"She was crying hysterically," Brianna said, her testimony almost word-for-word from the previous trial. "She couldn't get the words out."

"Did she tell you why she was so upset?" asked Livesay.

"Yes."

"Tell this jury what she told you."

That's when Truslow did something he didn't do in the first trial. He objected. He argued that anything Heather would have said to Brianna fell under inadmissible hearsay.

To the shock of the prosecution, the judge sustained the objection. Nothing Heather said—about Sidney leaving his wife, about wanting to meet her in the middle of the night—would be heard by the jury.

Livesay seemed momentarily stunned. She asked to address the court. The jury was sent out. She pressed Judge Dennis on why he allowed that testimony in the first trial, but not this one.

The reason, he said, was simple: "With the testimony of this witness in the earlier trial, there was no objection. Had there been, I'd have ruled the exact same way, no question about it. In fact, I will tell you this: I thought, 'Why in the world wasn't there an objection?' But there wasn't."

Livesay tried to argue that the judge wasn't remembering the first trial correctly. She also said the statement fell under one of the exceptions to the hearsay rule, the one allowing so-called "excited utterances."

The judge held firm. "I'm erring on the side of caution," he said. "I'll stand by my ruling."

Deflated, the prosecutor had little more to ask Warrelmann.

"Did she call you back that night?"

"No," she said.

The rest of the trial was replay: Heather's date Stephen Schiraldi, Tilted Kilt manager Jessica Cooke and cell phone records. There was no testimony about the surveillance video of the truck, since it fell outside the scope of the obstruction charge.

It was a quick, three-day trial, one that the defense could believe mostly went as well as could be expected. This left them with the same decision they'd faced before: Should Sidney take the stand in his own defense? As the television interview showed, he had things he wanted to say, corrections to be made. But silence seemed to work in the previous trial.

Sidney and his attorney grappled with the matter up until the very last moment, when the judge asked the defense on Wednesday, "Have you made a decision?"

"Yes, your honor," said Truslow.

"What is that decision?"

Sidney said, "I'm going to forgo my testimony."

His voice cracked and the words stammered out.

The judge said, "You certainly have indicated you were thinking about it. You know you have the absolute right to do that?"

"Yes, sir," he said quietly.

"And as we said, if you did, you would be subject to cross-examination. But you absolutely have the right to remain silent as you've already heard me tell this jury when we started, that they don't look to you to put on any evidence. And I will instruct them accordingly in my closing instruction, and reiterate that they can't even discuss it. And they can't use that against you. You understand that. But it is your right to testify, you understand that?"

"Yes, sir."

"Is anything affecting your decision today?"

Sidney buried his head in his hands and began to cry. "A lot of things."

"I understand it's emotional, and as I said, if this was something that would be a surprise I would probably take a recess and let you regroup and think and have some time. But this is something that you've addressed before. I understand that the die is cast, so to speak at the moment. It is your desire though to remain silent?

"Yes, sir."

"Are you under the influence of any alcohol or medication here today?"

"No, sir," he said, shaking his lowered head.

"And are you comfortable with the manner in which you had with your lawyers and the manner with which they've advised you on these issues?"

After a long pause, he said, "Yes, sir."

"Let the record reflect there was a hesitancy," said the judge. "I understand that. If you agree with everything your lawyers have done and made you happy, they probably haven't done their job."

The judge offered a last warning. Sidney could still change his mind up until the point the judge brought back in the jury.

"This is going to happen fairly quickly, as you already witnessed before," the judge said. Sidney reiterated his decision not to testify.

The judge was right. The pace of the already swift trial quickened. Livesay handled closing arguments again, delivering a smoother, more polished summation than she had the first time, asserting that "everything he told the police" was misleading as investigators searched for Heather. "Everything that came out of his mouth was some twisted version of the truth."

Truslow countered that the prosecution had taken a couple of minor missteps by Sidney and blew them up into a major obstruction of justice case because police had so fumbled the investigation they had no one else to blame. "They have resorted at this point to put anybody in jail for anything associated with this," said Truslow. "It's a whole bunch of crap!

"The power is with you, so please, for the love of everything, please, it's the only thing that works from keeping someone who's innocent from being found guilty," Truslow said. "They've fumbled this thing for four years in ways you and I can't imagine," he said. "It's causing trouble. It's causing pain. So they have resorted, at this point, to put anybody in jail for anything associated with this. Somebody's going to pay. They don't care who."

The jury was sent out. No notes, no drama, no Allen Charges. In 50 minutes, they had a verdict. The judge brought them into the courtroom for the reading of their decision.

Some say a speedy deliberation favors the defense; O.J. Simpson would certainly agree, acquitted after an eight-month trial before his lawyers had time to get a cup of coffee. Others say it favors the prosecution, certitude of guilt leaving no reason for discussion. In reality, there's probably no pattern.

As Sidney hung his head, the verdict was read:
Guilty.
As quickly as it started, it ended. Sidney's legal winning streak had come to a crashing halt. It was the first conviction in the county's most sensational, closely watched, heavily scrutinized, violently debated criminal cases.

The verdict, on Aug. 30, 2017, wasn't the murder conviction the authorities had once sought and certainly felt was deserved, but it was something. The judge asked if the defense wanted the jury polled. Truslow said yes. One by one, the jurors affirmed it. They believed he had obstructed justice in the disappearance of Heather Elvis.

All that was left was the penalty, and again, no time was wasted. Dennis called a hearing and Holford predictably requested the maximum penalty of 10 years in prison.

"We're not talking about a speeding ticket in this case. We're not talking about obstructing justice for something small. We're talking about a missing person. A young, 20-year-old female who was missing," he said. "He misled the police, and in doing so, here we are today, four years later, and this young girl has still not been found."

Truslow asked for the "low-end" term, even allowing Sidney to remain on his ankle monitor and home confinement, so he could work and support his family. "I think it's been way more difficult for him than many, many other people in home detention. He has had to relocate to Florida just to get money to survive, to feed his kids."

The judge, who had already slapped Sidney with five months in jail for violating his gag order, was in no mood for mercy. He said he needed to send a message of deterrence to the public. "You delayed the process, you hindered the process. We can't have that going on in our community," he said.

Judge Dennis sentenced Sidney to the maximum of 10 years, minus one year for time already served. Dennis said: "I think it's a fair punishment for what's been done."

As Sidney was hauled back to jail, the reality of his situation seemed to at last register. He had dodged many bullets, avoiding arrest in the early weeks even though he was the only suspect, getting out of jail on bond with a free pass to leave the state, winning a mistrial on the kidnapping charge. Now he was staring down years, not months, in prison.

The best-case scenario called for at least four years behind bars if he stayed out of trouble and dedicated himself to work in jail. In his new mug shot, he was almost unrecognizable. His long hair and goatee had been shorn, leaving him nearly bald with stubble around the face and neck, a razor nick on his chin. His mouth was downturned. His blue eyes stared blankly into the camera. He looked lost.

The *Post and Courier* newspaper crunched the numbers from the South Carolina Judicial Department and found that the state rarely charges anybody with obstruction of justice and, when it does, rarely gets convictions.

An average of 160 such cases were filed each year over the previous five years. Of the total, only seven ended with guilty verdicts. Usually, prosecutors dropped the cases altogether or negotiated pleas. Out of the 800 cases over that five-year period, only 28 percent resulted in guilty pleas, well below the 41 percent rate for all criminal charges.

A lot of that is because the law is so vague, so hard to prove or disprove, the guarantee of a conviction so uncertain, that prosecutors hardly bother to litigate—unless they have other motives.

In any other case, the charge probably would have been dropped once the judge split it off from the kidnapping count into a separate trial. In any other case, a jury might have spent 50 minutes to vote for acquittal, then grumble about the government wasting their time.

But as so many in Horry County have found repeatedly, the Heather Elvis disappearance was not just another case.

Interviewed by reporters after the trial, Heather's family expressed no joy in the outcome. That a man was sent to jail brought them no closer to finding her. At least two more trials loomed, weeks spent on hard wooden benches reliving the ordeal, more tears, more embarrassment, more anger and frustration.

It would be a long wait. The next trial was more than a year away. It gave Sidney Moorer ample time to decide whether to turn on his wife.

21.

For the next 14 months, the Heather Elvis case receded from the daily headlines as the Horry County Police Department shifted focus to other investigations and its own internal crisis.

In January of 2018, former Detective Allen Large, suffering a host of health issues, including heart disease and kidney ailments, was found dead in his home of what was determined to be natural causes. He was 55.

At the time, he was still facing criminal charges. As three of the five civil cases were settled with monetary payouts to the women, more details emerged. "He made me touch him, attempt to give him oral sex, but he was obsessed with giving me oral sex," one woman alleged in court papers obtained by WMBF-TV. "I felt so dirty. He also made me rub him with massage oil. He would show up in the middle of his work shift, wearing his gun and badge, asking for sex."

Not even the threat of getting caught stopped Large: "He said he was a bad man and that he was going to prison for a long time. I didn't understand. He said that he had done bad things to women for a long time and he was going to prison for a long time."

With the search for Heather long since suspended and no new investigative leads coming in, the only developments were legal maneuvers.

In April 2018, prosecutors secured a new indictment, adding conspiracy charges to the kidnapping counts. The

Solicitor's Office also tried to merge the two kidnapping cases into one, saying that trying Sidney and Tammy at the same trial would be more efficient since the witnesses and evidence were essentially the same. But the Supreme Court rejected the request. Justice Donald Beatty said the cases should be handled in "ordinary fashion."

Tammy's lawyers, meantime, requested that her trial be moved out of Horry County, as Sidney's was, but the judge assigned to her case, Circuit Court Judge Benjamin Culbertson, said the case would remain in his courtroom in Conway. In a nod to the potential taint from publicity, however, Culbertson granted a request to sequester the witnesses, barring them the courtroom and forbidding them to watch trial proceedings streaming on local news websites. This came at the request of the defense and would blow up in their face.

Lawyers spent six hours on Monday, Oct. 8, 2018, questioning potential jurors, settling on a panel of seven men and women. The judge welcomed the panel and braced them for a rigorous task ahead, telling them to clear their schedules until 6:30 every night. The judge also previewed the witness list, ticking off several members of both families, including Sidney Moorer.

Although it was still uncertain whether one side or the other would call Tammy's husband, now residing 87 miles to the west at the Lee Correctional Institution in Bishopville, the announcement sent small shockwaves through the courtroom. Sidney's attorney had all but accused Tammy in the first trial. Would Sidney do so himself, under oath?

With the legal housekeeping in order, the judge ordered everybody to return the next day for opening statements.

It was a different judge, two new attorneys at the prosecution and defense tables, but the same tension in the courtroom. Assistant Solicitor Christopher Helms, a big bear of a lawyer with a buzz cut and goatee, delivered the opening statement in a Southern twang. "I'm not going to beat a dead horse this morning. I'm not going to inundate you with all the information that I possibly could about this case," he began. "In my experience, the longer an attorney speaks during in the course of an opening statement, the weaker his position, or her position really is."

Borrowing the verbiage almost verbatim from the defense opening in Sidney Moorer's first trial wasn't the only mind game Helms had in store. More theatrical than the previous prosecutors, Helms stretched out his arm and pointed at Tammy Moorer, dramatically stating that she and her husband Sidney "conspired, planned and executed that plan to kidnap the victim in this case, Heather Elvis."

"Why are we here?" he asked the jury. "Well I'm going to show you why we are here." Helms then put a large portrait of Heather on an easel only feet away from the jury. "We are here because she can't be. She would like to be, I promise you, but she can't be."

Helms strolled over toward the defense table. "She can't be here because *she*"—he pointed to Tammy—"decided she can't be here on Dec. 18, 2013."

From there, Helms went through the now-familiar prosecution case, from the affair with Sidney, through the phone records, the surveillance video of the truck and the ugly text messages to Heather, only this time, the prosecutor portrayed Tammy as the instigator and driving force in a conspiracy to abduct her husband's young mistress.

"Tammy lays down the law. She puts on the pants in the family and Sidney is on probation," Helms said. "She takes his phone. He can't go to work alone anymore. She even chains him to the bed at night. I'm not speaking figuratively to you right now. Literally chains him to the bed at night."

Once it got out that Heather might be pregnant, "the fire, the jealousy that is in Tammy Moorer explodes into utter rage," Helms said. "This is the straw that breaks the camel's back. It's one thing to have an affair with my husband. It's one thing for you to humiliate me in this town. But it is an absolute whole other animal for you to be carrying the child from my husband. This is unacceptable. This is where the pain starts. This is where the conspiracy is formed."

Addressing the elephant in every courtroom, Helms said, "Obviously, the next question on our mind is: What do they do with her?"

Helms threw up his hands. "I don't know. We don't know. Law enforcement does not know," he said. "Three people know. She knows"—he gestured at Heather's photo—"wherever she is. Sidney Moorer knows. And that woman right over there"—another finger at Tammy—"knows."

He concluded his summation and took a seat, leaving the portrait of Heather looking at the jury. It forced attorney Casey Brown, as he approached jury for the defense summation, into the awkward position of dismantling the easel and placing Heather's picture facedown against the side of the jury box.

The symbolism was powerful: Tammy had allegedly made Heather disappear once, and through her attorney, she was doing it again.

It was an uncomfortable debut for Brown. The new face in the case was a boyish one. He had some theatrics of his own, holding before the jury wooden blocks.

"Square peg, round hole: Ever hear that expression?" he asked the jury as he fiddled with his blocks. "This doesn't fit, no matter how hard you try to wiggle it. Push it, force it, it doesn't fit. That's what the government is trying to do in this case. The government doesn't want us to look at this case objectively. The government is trying to make Tammy a scapegoat."

From there, he followed a common defense script of saying that the case was rife with reasonable doubt, then sought to define the concept. "Is it reasonable to think that aliens, the Russians had something to do with this?" he asked. "No. But is it reasonable to think that someone else did and she didn't? Yes."

Pointing out the prosecution shortcomings as defense lawyers had before—the lack of DNA, fingerprints and other physical evidence, the lack of clarity in the surveillance video of the truck—Casey said the case against Tammy crumbled.

He was so sure, he said, that Tammy herself would take the stand. "She's been waiting for the truth to be told, to finally get this over with," he said. "You have the power in this case to finally put an end to this."

As he finished, Tammy was in tears.

For what it was worth, Casey spoke for 11 minutes. Helms, who promoted the shorter-is-better theory, 22 minutes.

As forecast, the first part of the prosecution's case offered the same witnesses as Sidney's trial. Members of the Tilted Kilt staff were back, as was Stephen Schiraldi. Cpl. Furr and Officer Canterbury returned, and so did representatives of the cell phone companies to introduce records of the calls. For trial watchers, each round of testimony was as familiar as the next, and all expectations were focused on the upcoming appearance of Tammy Moorer.

The first new witness to testify was a Realtor named Laura Garlitz, called on Wednesday, Oct. 10, by the prosecution to dish on her friend, Tammy. Garlitz said Tammy was known to drink and smoke pot and admitted that she had her own boyfriend while Sidney was messing around with Heather.

Indeed, later in the trial, one of the more colorful witnesses took the stand. Kevin Michael Hummel was a 48-year-old New Jersey man with long hair and a modest résumé as a musician. "Pretty low level," he testified. "Bar gigs, theater work, nothing much. Probably never would have heard of me."

Tammy, though, knew all about him. They first met back in 1988 when he was vacation in South Carolina to celebrate his high school graduation. Twenty-five years later, they reconnected on Facebook and began a steamy online relationship exchanging X-rated texts.

"Basically, it was essentially, like, sexual in nature," he said. "I was single. She was looking for somebody to basically have sex with. I was all about that. That was pretty much what everything was about."

They never consummated their relationship in person, but texted throughout 2013, including on the day that Heather Elvis disappeared. He said they stopped after Heather went missing and had not been in contact since.

Another man in Tammy's life was barely a man at all, but an 18-year-old named Caleb with whom Tammy also exchanged explicit text messages. According to an investigator who uncovered them, the sexting started after Tammy discovered Sidney's affair and searched the Internet for the "cougar life."

"I want you Caleb," said one of Tammy's texts, read in court by the detective. "You don't even know. I want to fuck the hell out of you."

The young man took the witness stand to confirm the texts and say they stopped when his mother found out.

The evidence came in over strenuous defense objection. An outraged Greg McCollum called the texts "the most blush-worthy language I've ever experienced" and demanded a mistrial. The judge denied the motion.

Another new round of evidence came from former Horry County Sheriff's Office investigator Carmen Rodriguez, who recounted one of her meetings with Tammy Moorer. This happened when the harassment had started getting out of control and Tammy wanted the sheriff's office to do something about it. Tammy had just gone on Facebook to dismiss her husband's relationship as nothing more than her husband's romp in the backseat of Heather's car.

Rodriguez told Tammy that the relationship was more serious. To prove it, she showed Tammy something detectives had found in her car, evidence that until now the public hadn't know about: a motel room key. Detectives tracked down the motel and retrieved a receipt. It was for a room that Sidney had rented for a liaison with Heather.

Tammy, the former rock 'n' roll photographer, pulled out her camera and snapped a picture of the room key, said Rodriguez.

According to Rodriguez, Tammy also acknowledged knowing more about Heather than had been previously disclosed. Rodriguez went over those final phone calls from Heather's cell phone to Sidney's the night she disappeared. In the one that Sidney answered while he had said, they were in, Tammy could hear—and recognize—Heather's voice.

"She told me she heard Heather's voice on the phone call, so she knew it was her," Rodriguez testified. Apparently sensing how bad that might make her look, Tammy then backpedaled. "Initially, she said that Heather Elvis had made the call," said Rodriguez. "A little bit later, she came up with the theory maybe those were spoof calls."

A former Tilted Kilt manager, Dennis Clark, recalled how an angry Tammy called one day—he couldn't narrow the date any more than it was between October and December 2013—demanding that Heather be fired or Tammy's husband would stop working there. "Tammy barged into the conversation and proceeded to tell me how Heather was causing problems for her family, spreading rumors that she was pregnant by her husband and to fire her," Clark testified. He never did fire Heather and never met Tammy in person.

The prosecution called Jill Domogauer, a crime scene investigator with the Horry County Police Department who had testified before, and for a time, it appeared that it would be more of the same. She spoke of processing Heather's car and finding no fingerprints or DNA from Tammy. There were also no weapons or drug paraphernalia. Just a lot of trash of no evidentiary value. Nothing was found at Peachtree Landing, either, save for cigarette butts that proved meaningless, nor at the Moorers' home two months later after they were arrested.

Something did turn up at Heather's apartment, however. Her place, like her car, was cluttered, and Domogauer saw no signs of forced entry, no trace of a struggle, no drugs. The cell phone and keys weren't there. She spotted the empty suitcase in Heather's room, personal items and toiletries of the sort one would be inclined to pack if leaving, and one very important discovery in the bathroom.

In the trashcan was the box to a pregnancy test. The test stick was missing.

This had never been revealed before, and why it didn't come up at Sidney's trial was not known.

It seemed that much of the trial now was racing toward Tammy's testimony, the prosecution doing everything it could to lay the groundwork for what would promised to be a grueling cross-examination.

Heather's roommate, Brianna Warrelmann, returned for her third go-around and said that pregnancy test didn't belong to her. She again recounted her last conversation with Heather—the testimony wasn't blocked this time. She said she'd never met Sidney's wife, but knew that Heather was "scared of Tammy." Asked by Nancy Livesay if she had spoken to Heather again, Brianna's voice cracked and she said, "I haven't."

The seventh day of trial was the last for the prosecution's case. Sidney would not be testifying, at least not for the prosecution. Instead, Livesay called his mother, Irene H. Moorer. The very picture of Southern decorum, Irene calmly answered in a soft voice gentle questions from the prosecutor, stating her hometown in South Carolina, saying she had been married for 50 years to husband Larry, and giving her age as 69.

"I would have never guessed that," Livesay said. She then asked if Irene knew Tammy Moorer. She said she did.

"How do you know Tammy?"

"She's married to my youngest son, Sidney. I've known her since they got together—20 years or so."

"After Tammy and Sidney got married, tell me, was Sidney allowed to come see you and your husband by himself?"

This prompted a quick defense objection and a sidebar meeting between lawyers and the judge, ending with Livesay slightly rephrasing her question.

"Did Sidney ever come down and see you by himself without Tammy?"

"Just once."

"And that was one time in over 20 years?"

Irene nodded sadly.

Livesay next asked her about Christmas Eve 2013—a week after Heather had gone missing and after Sidney had already spoken to police—when Sidney, Tammy and their children showed up at his parents' house unannounced. The evening ended with a long sit-down talk between Sidney, Tammy and his mother and father.

"Did Tammy say anything about the fact Sidney had had an affair?"

"Sidney made the comments."

The defense objected again, this time on hearsay grounds. She would not be allowed to recall what Sidney said, only Tammy.

"Tell this jury what Tammy told you she did to Sidney?"

"You want me to say that word?" said Irene, looking embarrassed. "She said she beat the hell out of him."

The penultimate witness for the prosecution was a wildcard: Donald DeMarino. Skinny, with a scruffy beard, a neck tattoo and a smoker's rasp, the 25-year-old DeMarino said he was the second cousin of Tammy Moorer and has "known her all my life."

"Has there ever been any bad blood between you or disagreements?" asked Livesay.

"Never," he said. "I was in their wedding."

He recalled that someday after Heather Elvis had gone missing—he couldn't remember exactly when—that he went with his grandmother to the home of "Aunt Polly"—Tammy's mother—for a family function. Tammy and Sidney were there.

"Did you see a picture of Heather Elvis at that house?"

"Yes."

"What did you see that picture on?"

"A phone."

"What kind of phone did you see it on?"

"Boost mobile phone, flip phone."

Livesay's next questions were cryptic and carefully framed. This portion of his testimony had been ruled inadmissible at a previous trial by Judge Dennis.

"When you saw that picture of Heather Elvis, in that picture, could she move at all?"

"I don't think so."

"Did it look like she could talk?"

"No."

"After you saw the picture, what did you do?"

"Nothin'. I didn't know what to do."

"Did you stay at the house or did you leave?"

"I left."

"How did you feel when you saw the picture?"

"I don't know. I really don't know."

"At any point, did you tell the police what you saw on that phone?"

"It wasn't until later I told."

"Who was the first person you told?"

He pointed to a staff person from the Solicitor's Office in the courtroom.

"After you talked to her, did we promise you anything in exchange for telling us?"

"No."

"Have you been in trouble, Don?"

"Yes, I've been in trouble." He had been arrested for burglary and breaking into cars.

"Has the Solicitor's Office ever done anything with you on those charges?"

"Never."

"Was what you're telling the jury today about what you saw on the phone true?"

"Yes, ma'am."

"Do you know why that picture was taken?"

"I believe for Tammy Moorer."

"After seeing that picture, do you expect anybody to hear from Heather Elvis?"

"No."

Greg McCollum approached for cross-examination.

"You've led kind of a tough life?"

"Yes, sir."

"Do you have a job?"

"Not at the moment."

He said been doing flooring work with a friend, but the jobs dried up and now he was unemployed. He estimated he worked two to four months this year, making $15 to $20 an hour, maybe two weeks the previous year.

"You know what taxes are?" asked McCollum.

"Yes."

"Did you file a tax return in 2017?"

"No, sir."

"Did you file a tax return in 2016?"

"No, sir."

"Did you file a tax return in 2015?"

"No."

"Have you ever filed a tax return?"

"No."

"You think that's illegal?"

"I know why I didn't."

"That's called breaking the law, isn't it?"

"I believe so."

"It's also a form of dishonesty?"

"If you say so, yes."

"You've used illegal drugs?"

"Yes."

"More times than you can remember?"

"Yes."

He said the first time he told somebody about the photo was when he was in jail in 2016 or 2017. He told a cellmate and the cellmate apparently told the Solicitor's Office, which got in touch with him.

"How do we know when you're lying and when you're not?" asked McCollum.

"You don't," said DeMarino.

It would be left to the jury to decide whether DeMarino really had seen a picture of a dead Heather Elvis.

The prosecution wrapped up its case by calling two more law enforcement witnesses. The first said that Heather's phone went dead at 3:41 a.m. on Dec. 18, 2013, and has not shown activity since. The second witness said she had been monitoring databases from the DMV, police departments and other agencies for any sign of Heather. The most recent review was two days earlier. Heather still did not come up.

On Wednesday, Oct. 18, the state rested.

22.

The defense case got off to a disastrous start.

One of Tammy Moorer's intended witnesses was her eldest son. He was going to testify that he saw her in their home around the time prosecutors alleged she was out kidnapping Heather Elvis. Prosecutors, who already said the Moorer children had been "coached," had prepared a sharp cross-examination, and it was questionable how much stock any jury would put in the world of a defendant's loving child who could lose his mother to jail.

His testimony became moot when a court officer opened the door to the courthouse room where witnesses were being sequestered to find Tammy's son, at least one other child and mother Polly Caison watching live stream of the trial on a man's laptop in apparent violation of the judge's order prohibiting witnesses from watching the trial until they completed their testimony. The officer confiscated the laptop, and alerted the judge.

The judge summoned Tammy's son to the stand for a hearing in which he denied watching the trial. He said he was busy on his phone watching YouTube videos. He wasn't supposed to have a phone, either, and prosecutor Helms warned him, "You know that on that stand, you have to tell the truth? If you don't, that's illegal." He said he understood that, but he insisted he hadn't seen the trial.

The judge didn't believe him: "I find that the officer's testimony was credible."

The judge barred as witnesses the son, his siblings, Tammy's mother—who also was prepared to provide alibi testimony—and another woman in the room for violating the sequestration arrangement that Tammy's lawyers had originally requested.

That left only one relative—her sister, Ashley—to testify for Tammy. Ashley recounted how on the night of Heather Elvis's disappearance, Tammy accompanied Sidney on his work duties while Ashley watched the children at their parents' house adjacent to Tammy's home.

At 3:10 a.m., she got the text, "Home," from Tammy and responded, "Awake and up."

She awakened the children, ushered them out of the house, and watched them walk across the lawn until they got to their home, meeting Tammy and Sidney who were still unlocking the front door. Ashley then went back to her parents' house and sorted coupons for most of the night, exchanging Facebook posts with Tammy across the lawn.

Nancy Livesay handled the cross-examination in what would be a tune-up for the confrontation with Tammy. She began by asking about the text messages she exchanged on Nov. 11, 2013, from the Tilted Kilt in which Tammy requested a picture.

"I'm assuming this is the young lady you were looking for?" said Livesay, holding up a portrait of Heather.

"I wasn't looking for anyone. We had a drink at Tilted Kilt."

"Tell the jury," Livesay asked again, "is this the woman you were looking for?"

"That is who she is referring to. I was not looking for anyone. My sister is not in there and I was not in there looking for her."

"Even before you knew that Sidney and Heather had had an affair?"

"Yes."

"How did you know what she looked like?"

"Facebook."

"So you looked her up on Facebook?"

"Through Facebook. I never met her."

"You knew that she worked at Tilted Kilt?"

"Yes."

Quoting Tammy's response that she thought "the bitch was in hiding," Livesay asked, "Why did she think she was in hiding?"

"My sister has a horrible vocabulary."

She acknowledged telling police that Tammy had handcuffed Sidney to the bed, but told Livesay it was part of sex play, not punishment for the affair. Livesay showed her the statement to the police in which she said it was punishment, and asked, "So you did see Sidney handcuffed to the bed?"

"No, because there's no way to handcuff him to the bed."

"You were lying?"

"No, I wasn't lying. I haven't seen him handcuffed to the bed."

She said it was a sleigh bed and there was no place on which to latch the cuffs. When shown more of her statement to police, she finally said, "I don't remember this interview very well. If I said it, I said it."

Taking Ashley through the early morning of Dec. 18, 2013, she repeated that shortly after the 3:10 a.m. text from her sister, "I went to the door. The truck was there. And they were both there on the porch waiting for the children to walk across." But she acknowledged she received no more texts from her sister until 7:02 the next morning.

The defense next called a man who said he'd met Heather Elvis in early 2013 and had a sexual relationship with her. When Casey Brown asked if the man felt like he was "pursued" by Heather, the prosecution objected and the judge shut down the questioning. On cross-examination, he said he had last seen Heather in April 2013 and had no idea what happened to her.

The defense also brought in Heather's friend, who gave her a place to live in 2012 after she came to work one day with a bruise on her neck. Heather didn't want to go home and didn't want her family to know what happened. The friend said Heather was welcome at the apartment, but she couldn't bring her boyfriend at the time. Under cross-examination, the friend said she hadn't seen Heather since 2012 and knew nothing personally about Sidney Moorer.

Another witness had even less to say about Heather: a man who knew her briefly and hadn't talked to her for about a year before she disappeared.

And the defense brought in Evan German, the tipster who thought he spotted Heather in a bar after she went missing. He recounted how Heather and Brianna would come to his beach house for parties. When Brown asked if they smoked pot, the judge sustained a prosecution objection that the question was irrelevant. On the Friday after Heather's disappearance, he hugged a woman at the Beaver Bar he thought was her.

"I was mistaken."

"Who told you you were mistaken?"

"The video evidence showed that you couldn't see the tattoo on her arm, so it wasn't her."

"At the time you were so sure you told police?"

"I thought I did," he said. "I drank too much that night. … I was under the influence of alcohol that night, so my judgment was off."

As Heather's father listened to this testimony about his daughter, he seethed. Soon Terry Elvis's emotions would get the best of him.

In the final walkup to Tammy's testimony, the defense called a hospital official to testify that records showed that Tammy Moorer had a positive pregnancy test on March 25, 2014, while she was in jail. The officials acknowledged under cross-examination that the records could be incomplete and that they couldn't comment in detail on her medical condition since they were record keepers, not physicians.

Defense attorney Greg McCollum then told the judge: "Your honor, at this time, the defense calls Tammy Moorer."

Tammy had bleached blond hair and wore a long black sweater over a fuchsia blouse. On Oct. 19, she took the oath to tell the truth, sat in the witness chair and smiled at the jury.

Under friendly questioning by her own attorney, Tammy opened her testimony by portraying herself as a proud member of the Horry County community, born and raised the area. "I've lived on the property that's in question since 1974," she said. "My parents bought it. They started out with a trailer and built their lives. They built a bigger home."

She was the daughter of William. "He passed away while I was incarcerated," she said. She pointed to a woman in the courtroom. "My mother is right here," Polly, a gospel singer in church who waitressed at a resort hotel in Myrtle Beach. "They worked really hard to get what they have over the years," she said. "I've just been there with them up until all of this happened, then I couldn't live here anymore."

She introduced Ashley, "my only sister," and recalled the sacrifices she made for her, looking after her instead of studying journalism. She beamed as she introduced her children, her 12-year-old son "on the far left, over there," and her older son, next to Tammy's mother. She said, "He's already out on his own in college, got a full-time job. He's way ahead of where I was. I'm very proud of him." She spoke of her daughter, too. She spoke of how Tammy and her husband homeschooled her children. "Up until this happened," she said, "they were straight-A students."

"Did that change after you were arrested and went to jail?" asked McCollum.

"It did. My kids became very depressed. They did their work, but at the beginning—and I don't want to get her upset, so I'll be brief with it—but as soon as I was arrested, I was denied bond, and one week after I was denied bond, my father passed away and it destroyed my family."

As Tammy began to softly cry, McCollum asked, "Do you know where your father's funeral was?"

"At the church where—," she said, weeping.

"Do you know the name of the church, the denomination?"

"It was a Baptist church," she said through tears.

"As far as you know, that's where your father's funeral was?"

"I wasn't able to attend."

While she missed her father's funeral, the sheriff's department took her and Sidney to the funeral home at different times to pay their last respects.

"With a police escort?"

"Yes, in chains and shackles with my hands tied behind my back and my feet were tied together," she sobbed.

"Was anybody else there beside the funeral home people and the body of your father and the guards?"

"No."

"Were any of your family members there?"

"No."

It was, she said, one more insult during incarceration at the Georgetown County sheriff's jail, where she claimed guards forced her to sleep on the floor, even though she'd taken a pregnancy test and believed she was carrying a child, which at age 42 was risky enough, but worse for her because she'd already had one miscarriage and took prenatal vitamins that made her bleed. Her words tumbling out, as if she could finally expose the indignities she's suffered, she talked of being shackled and sent by van to the hospital, where she was given an ultrasound after missing a period, and how even though she had been trying to get pregnant during her family trip to California and had taken several pregnancy tests, at first the "hospital didn't believe I was pregnant."

Finally, "They ran a lot of tests with blood and that."

"Did they also conclude that you were pregnant?"

"Yes, they did."

"Did they give you the literature and stuff that tells you how to have a good pregnancy?"

"I was given the ABCs of pregnancy. I was given a follow-up appointment with an ob-gyn. That's when they started fussing back and forth with me because I wanted to see my doctor who was familiar with my situation and they refused to let me see him. I went to court to try to get out of jail based on pregnancy. And I was denied a second bond at that time."

"You never delivered a baby did you?"

"I did not. I lost the baby."

She said the jail never so much as gave her a follow-up doctor's appointment.

And so it went for Tammy. She was finally released on bail, but had to move.

"We were here for a little bit, but there was a lot of hatred, stalking," she said, turning and speaking directly to the jurors. "It's not the community, let me be clear. There was another side to this. There was a side where we would go out and people would say, 'We're sorry this is happening to you. We love your family. Let us do good things for you.' They would give us free food in restaurants. There was a lady who would come to our house and bring us groceries because we couldn't work. We had people buying me clothes, buying my daughter clothes, buying my little boy toys, video games, things like that.

"We had a lot of support in this community, a lot. The only time I ever had anything happen to us was one time we were at Sam's Club and a lady shouted a nasty, derogatory word in front of all of us. That was the only negative thing that had happened physically to me. Everyone else would come out and help my family. My mom had tons of support. We still do.

"But our supporters are scared to show up in this courtroom because of the threats that are made on our supporters. I just want y'all to know that."

She described life in Florida, their family crammed into a "little camper" while she had to wear an ankle bracelet. "It's on me right now, an ankle monitor," she said. "I have to take a drug test, you have to pee for them, they have to see you in person to make sure you still have it in. They make sure they have tabs on you."

Sidney could keep working, she said, but not in Horry County. "They did want to hire him, but they didn't want all of this media and all of the threats that were coming from people—they were under fake names. They would harass the restaurants.

"I didn't want my mama to have to suffer working paying for my family to survive. And these employers that you're talking about, certain ones, like Olive Garden, they loved Sidney. He always did a good job for them."

The children fell behind in school, "but they caught up quickly." She went back to work waiting tables, but somebody saw her face on a television crime show and "I was terminated," which was a disaster because her husband "is in prison right now. I had to work to support him."

Finally, prosecutor Nancy Livesay stood and said, "Your honor, I'm just concerned how is this relevant to the trial we're here today for?"

The judge asked McCollum to get back on track.

"At some point," the lawyer asked Tammy, "did you come to believe that your husband, Sidney, was having an affair?"

"Yes, it was Halloween night going into Nov. 1, that morning. That's when I found out."

"When you found out that he was having an affair, did you know who he was having the affair with?"

"I did not."

"Did you know if he was having an affair with a woman or a man?"

"I did not. He led me to believe it was a gay. He told me it was a man."

"What were your concerns about him having an affair and you not knowing about it?"

She began by recalling a day in 2012 when Sidney sent pictures of himself to someone "and they were doing dirty text messages, that type of thing," when Livesay objected again.

"That's actions of Sidney Moorer. Today is not Sidney's trial."

"Overruled, I'll allow that."

Tammy said that after those dirty texts, which were, in fact, to a woman, "I told him after that, he had broken the trust of my family. He didn't have sex with the girl, but it was enough. To me, it was cheating, going outside the marriage, at that time, and it kind of hurt my children and at that time I kind of considered a divorce from him. But it wasn't really that big of a deal. He didn't have sex with anyone. Stupidly, I forgave him. You know, I thought he wouldn't do it again, and next thing I know, I'm getting the text messages from someone else and he's trying to hide them."

"What kind of text messages were you seeing?"

"I didn't see that, but I knew he was getting one because he would put the phone down. But they were deleted. I never saw them."

"So he was acting suspicious?"

"He was right beside me."

"And when was this again?"

"We had went to bed. I think we were watching TV and the phone went off and he just put it down. You wouldn't hide a work call."

"And did you go behind his back and look at the phone and try to determine what's going on?"

"No, I asked him to see the phone."

"And did he show it to you?"

"He had already deleted it, so it wasn't there to see."

"Were you mad?"

"I was suspicious. I didn't know what he was hiding. I didn't know if he was planning. Sidney would plan things all the time and do surprising things for me or for the kids. So I was just making sure it wasn't something in relation to that. Eventually, he will tell you. He's honest. He'll look at you and tell you something's up if you look at him in the eyes, he'll tell you, and he told me that it was B.J., a guy."

This brought another objection, for hearsay, which the judge sustained.

"At some point, did you learn who he was having the affair with?"

"Not until the girl called me back and told me who she was," Tammy explained, saying that was later. At the time, "I had no idea. So the messages were never directed toward Heather Elvis. They were directed to the mystery person. I just wanted to know who it was."

"And did you feel like you had a right to know who it was?"

"I did. I didn't go about it the right way, and I'm sorry for that. It looks bad. But I just wanted to know who it was. That's all."

"You've been known to use some pretty salty language?"

"Right."

"And you're one to show your emotions around people?"

"I am."

Within hours after that flurry of "time to meet the Mrs." texts, Heather called her back. "She was a nice girl. She told me everything that had happened. And when Sidney came home, I asked him to confirm it to see what his side of the story was. Heather told me she and Sidney were really good friends."

"After you spoke to her, did your impression toward her soften?"

"Yes."

"Did you know her prior to speaking with her?"

"No, I've never met her."

Moving to the early part of the investigation, Tammy said she and Sidney cooperated with police. "I wanted them to leave us alone and go find out what really happened to her instead of wasting time with my family," she said.

They went voluntarily to the police station where she spoke alone with Detective Allen Large. "He took his own interview," she said. "They wanted to see if our stories were different. They were the same. I have a recording of it here today." (It would not be played.)

She told Large everything she and Sidney had done the night Heather was missing, but Large manhandled Sidney and wouldn't let him get an attorney.

That drew another objection—for hearsay. The defense had already challenged the police statements on Miranda grounds and lost.

"At some point, you determined you were going to leave, correct?"

"Yes."

"The police did not stop you from leaving?"

"They tried to."

"But eventually?"

"Yes."

She left Sidney at the police station, where he gave the interview to detectives Martin and Cauble, while she went to her parents' house. Police cars were parked in front. She had not told her parents yet. Before she could warn them, officers were knocking on their door.

She said police later seized their Ford F-150 truck, twice, and searched it, finding cement mix, a trowel, and a five-gallon bucket.

"Were there any efforts made to try to hide those materials?"

"No."

"Did you or anyone to your knowledge use some kind of concrete to try to bury a body?"

Tammy turned to the jury. "Never."

"Did you or somebody in your family to your knowledge use some kind of tile cleaner or cleaning fluid to try to clean up some kind of crime scene?"

"Never."

"Did you or anyone in your family to your knowledge use cleaning fluid to try to clean out your house?"

"No."

"Did you or anyone to your knowledge use cleaning fluid to try to scrub up and clean out your truck?"

"Never. The truck's dirty."

"Doesn't that seem like kind of a preposterous question to ask you?"

"You have to ask it. We're in court."

McCollum next brought her through the family trip to Disneyland in the fall of 2013, after she discovered the affair. He asked why she didn't cancel it.

"I was angry with Sidney for about 72 hours and then I was over it. And it may sound impossible, but it was."

She denied, as the prosecution had alleged, that she forced Sidney to get a tattoo with her name on it. She produced a photo of Sidney getting the tattoo dated in 2012, long before he met Heather Elvis. Nor, she said, did she ever handcuff her husband to the bed in retaliation for the affair, though the couple did use handcuffs in sex play.

"Do you own a set of—I don't know—novelty handcuffs?"

"We each have that. I'm not comfortable talking about it with strangers, but yes, we would play with those at times."

She said police seized Sidney's pair, but left hers behind.

"With the novelty handcuffs, do you need a key to uncuff yourself?"

"No."

"You could just let yourself out of them?"

"You can. There's a little button you press and let you out."

"Did you ever own a set of real law enforcement handcuffs?"

"We did."

"You had to use a key to get them open?"

"Yeah."

"Did the police seize those?"

"I don't know."

"Do you know where they are?"

"I haven't looked for them."

"Did you ever use those to handcuff Sidney to the bed?"

"No, I have not."

"Did you ever handcuff him to the bed and leave him without the keys so Sidney couldn't get loose?"

"No, I have not. Sidney's a strong man. He can get out of anything."

She said she'd been to Peachtree Landing, but not the night that Heather Elvis disappeared.

"I've never been back," she said.

"To your knowledge, did anybody that you know or associate with you go to Peachtree Landing on the night of Dec. 17, 2013?"

"No."

"After midnight on Dec. 18, 2013, between the hours of, say, midnight and the next day, did you, yourself, go to Peachtree Landing?"

"No."

"Did anybody that you know or are associated with go to Peachtree Landing between midnight and, say, noon the next day?"

"No."

"To your knowledge, did somebody drive your F-150 black Ford pickup truck down 814 that night on the way to Peachtree Landing?"

"Not that I know."

Going over the night with Sidney, she said the couple went to the discount store Bi-Lo to get an advertisement—she and her sister planned to clip coupons the next day. As she and Sidney approached the house, she sent a text message to her sister at 3:10 a.m. when they got home. Sidney pulled the truck into the driveway. Her sister woke up the children; her older son was allowed to stay up and play Minecraft.

Sidney picked up the two younger children and brought them back to the house, where they stayed for the rest of the night except for one brief period later in the morning when Sidney went outside to feed the dogs. Tammy caught up on paperwork for her children's home schooling until about 4 a.m. and posted messages on Facebook.

Tammy gave much of the same account of the evening as Sidney did. "I worked with him. If it was something I could help him do, I would help him," she said. "I helped him do a lot of shopping. I helped him save money when we buy things." They went to Longhorn's and Sticky Fingers. They went to Bi-Lo to pick up the advertising flyer.

They went to Broadway on the Beach for "fooling around"—sex in the truck. "Right after we did that, there was a little bit of a mess," she said. "He went to a gas station to get stuff to clean that up."

"At this time, did you think there was an active relationship between Sidney Moorer—your husband—and Heather Elvis?"

"No."

"Did you think that ended?"

"Yes."

"Are you aware of a phone call that your husband made from a pay phone?"

"I am not aware. Sidney denies that to me."

"Do you remember your husband leaving your presence and going somewhere outside of the truck for about five minutes?"

"I do not."

At some point, they went to Walmart to get the pregnancy test.

"We had sex before Walmart and then we had sex again after the Walmart."

They then returned to Sticky Fingers to make sure the alarm code was set, then went to Bi-Lo to pick up an advertising flyer, then straight home.

Between 11 a.m. and noon, she got up to deal with a problem with her mother, who had gotten a flat tire. Sidney drove with the children to change the tire while Tammy stayed at home where she uploaded photos to Facebook from the Disneyland trip. "It was a normal day," she said.

"Did you fly into a rage and get in the truck and drive to the boat landing?"

"Of course not."

"Did Sidney say he had to go somewhere and get in the truck and leave?"

"No."

"Did anything out of the ordinary occur?"

"No."

It wasn't until the night of Dec. 19 that Sidney got the call from police. He was working with Tammy at Sticky Fingers. The detective told him police had found Heather's car. "That was the first time we heard about it," she said.

"Have you been living under this cloud for almost five years?"

"For almost five years now."

"Has that been easy?"

"No, it has not."

"Is this the first opportunity that you've had to publicly declare your innocence?"

"It is. I have a gag order on my case."

"Are you glad that you're able to tell people what happened and what you did do and didn't do?"

"I want people to know the truth. And I, too, want Heather found. I think she deserves to be found. And I think they botched her case and didn't do justice for Heather."

"That's all I have, your honor."

Nancy Livesay walked up and looked at Tammy Moorer.

"Miss Moore, do you know who I am?"

"I do."

"And who am I?"

"Nancy Livesay. You've made my life miserable."

23.

Tammy Moorer stared back at Nancy Livesay: "Am I allowed to ask you a question?"

The judge said, "No, ma'am."

"Sorry," said Tammy.

"Just respond to her," said the judge.

"Of course."

Livesay asked, "You do know who Heather Elvis is, correct?"

"I do. She is a very pretty girl."

"Just so we're on the same page," said Livesay, holding up a photo of Heather, "this is her?"

"Yes, it is."

"And is this the way you saw her?"

"I've never seen her. That's a picture, yes."

Nancy Livesay was in full attack mode. Never once did she start a question with her folksy, "If you don't mind." Facing off against Tammy Moorer seemed to mind very much.

Tammy said she had talked to her on the phone, however, when Heather dialed the number associated with the nasty text messages.

"She didn't hang up when she called me or anything," said Tammy. "It was a nice conversation. She was a nice girl. She wasn't mean to me. I wasn't mean to her."

"You were not mean to her?"

"I was not mean to her on that conversation," Tammy said, anticipating Livesay's next line of questioning. "Those messages you're about to read are not—it was over and done, Nancy, in two days."

"So when you sent: 'I frown upon people who hang up on me, not cool'—?"

"I didn't know who she was. I had not spoken to her. She didn't speak to me. I didn't know if it was man or a woman. I didn't know who that was."

Livesay read another text: "You can tell me who you are right now or I will find out another way. That way won't have a great turnout for you."

She asked, "You now know when you sent her that text she was a 20-year-old girl?"

"I know now, but I didn't know then."

"So you didn't care if she was 15 when you sent her that text? You didn't care if she was 16?"

"I didn't know who it was going to."

Livesay asked her about this text reply from Heather: "Nobody you need to worry about. Please leave me alone."

"That raised more questions for me," said Tammy, "because why would she say that? That made me think it was some sort of affair. I understand the way you're looking at it and the way the world's looked at it for five years. You guys didn't understand my point of view. My point of view was: I didn't know who I was talking to in the beginning. Once Heather told me the truth, I didn't care anymore."

Nancy asked about this text from Tammy: "It's best you call me back and speak immediately. Save yourself."

Tammy said, "Not in your tone of voice. It wasn't meant that way. It was meant to get the man or the woman or the monkey to call me back." She said that after she sent the text, "I'm giving you one last chance to answer before we meet," Heather called.

"And we're fine."

If that were so, Livesay asked, why did Tammy then send this message: "Hey sweetie, are you ready to meet the Mrs.?"

Tammy explained, "What you don't know, and what no one else has known until now because of the gag order, is that Heather Elvis and I had a conversation and she told me what had happened with Sidney. She was willing to meet me and my children."

"After that you wrote her, 'Hey sweetie are you ready to meet the Mrs.'?"

"I was referred to as 'The Missus' by the Tilted Kilt people. She told me."

Livesay then showed Tammy phone records from about 10 days later, on Nov. 11, when Tammy asked her sister in a text to "take a pic for me." Her sister responded, "She wasn't there," to which Tammy texted, "I think the bitch is in hiding."

Livesay asked, "Isn't that what you said?"

Tammy pointed to the records. "It's in there."

"What makes you think 'the bitch is in hiding'?"

"I guess I was just being a jerk, Nancy. That's all I can say."

Livesay asked, "Have we ever met outside of this courtroom?"

"I don't think so."

"I didn't know when we got on a first-name basis."

Livesay pressed ahead with more text messages, starting with the one on Dec. 6 to a friend in which Tammy wrote of Sidney: "I fucking hate him."

Tammy said that she was trying to make her marriage work for the sake of the children. "But I was also exploring other options at that time."

"That was while y'all were on this trip to rekindle the flames of love?"

"We were working on everything and Sidney was telling me a lot more about his childhood, that he had never told me before," she said. "I was just sort of like getting to know him a little bit better. I still hated him a lot. I hate him a lot now because he didn't stand up for himself and testify in his last trial. It's just—there's feelings for people. It's hard to overcome that."

"I understand."

Tammy added, "We were having a lot of sex."

"So you were obviously very angry?"

"I was back and forth with him."

"And this anger obviously lasted longer than 72 hours?"

"Not with Heather. With Sidney. Sidney's not the one missing. You're making it sound like we would hurt Heather, and it's not Heather."

Asked why, then, in a text to another friend after Heather went missing, Tammy called her a "psycho whore."

Tammy said at the time, she wasn't sure if Heather had really disappeared. "When that was posted we were being stalked and harassed by a group of people, and that group of people is in this courtroom today, and they also called Heather a prostitute, slut and a whore," said Tammy (It wasn't clear who she was talking about). "I regret it. I don't know if they do."

"Without a doubt, you were still angry?"

"I was mad," Tammy acknowledged. "I thought that she was in on it, at that time. I thought that she was doing it just to get back at him. I didn't know every single detail."

Tammy also explained that when she texted a friend on Dec. 7 that, "Now he had to stay chained to the bed until further notice while I live my life as a single mom," the text could be misconstrued.

"That's not the way it sounds. It's not a physical chain. You saw my bed. There's not a way to chain someone to my bed."

Livesay reminded Tammy that her own sister testified to seeing Sidney locked to something. "You remember that?"

"She testified to his fuzzy handcuffs, not to being locked to anything in my house. I never chained my husband to the bed, no."

"Were you lying to her?"

"Sure," Tammy responded with sarcasm in her voice, "I was lying to her."

Asked if she recalled looking up the phases for the moon on her computer on Dec. 15, she said, "I don't recall that."

"Do you know that the night that she was kidnapped was a full moon?"

"I do not."

And Livesay read yet another text to a friend, this on Dec. 16, the day before Heather disappeared, saying, "I guess we need to have a long talk so you know everything. I'm telling you, my heart has been black for a long time, about two years."

Tammy said that this was in response to the friend's insistence that Tammy remain married for the sake of the children.

"I still hate him sometimes. I'm not with him now. I moved on," Tammy said. "I love Sidney, but I'm not in love with Sidney."

Cross-examination ended for the day with Tammy being asked about her sex text messages to the New Jersey musician on Dec. 18. She said, "I was texting a man sexual messages while I was with Sidney, making love to my husband. I would come out and text another man. I made mistakes. We all make mistakes."

Everyone, she said, but Jesus Christ. "No one is perfect."

24.

After the weekend, Nancy Livesay and Tammy Moorer started off with small talk. They exchanged good mornings. Asked how their weekends were. Shared concerns that the dry weather was causing allergies to flare up.

Then it was back to battle. Livesay asked if Tammy had heard Heather's voice on the call to Sidney's phone the morning Heather disappeared. Tammy said she vaguely remembered the call, but didn't know how long it was or what time it came.

Livesay reminded her that phone records showed it was at 3:17 a.m. and lasted 261 seconds, ending at about 3:22 a.m. Livesay then said that 13 minutes later, at 3:45 a.m., the surveillance video captured the couple's Ford truck heading down Highway 814 toward Peachtree Landing.

"That's what you tell people," Tammy said.

"Do you remember Friday when the expert came in?" Livesay asked, referring to Grant Fredericks.

"I don't consider him an expert."

"Do you remember him saying it was your truck?"

"Of course I do. He was paid a lot of money."

Tammy said that at 3:36 a.m., she was at home Facebooking. The timestamp on her post proved it.

"He can say anything you pay him to say. My truck did not go to the landing that night. I promise you that on this Holy Bible." Tammy then put her hand on the Bible on which she took the oath minutes earlier. "I believe he was paid to lie."

"You agree it's a truck in the video?"

"There's a lot of trucks in the neighborhood. We live in the South. You can go out in the parking lot and know there's a million trucks. That's not my truck. That's the whole point here."

"But have you been in here for the testimony?"

"People lie, Nancy—I'm sorry, Miss Livesay. I don't know what to call you."

Livesay would return to that Facebook post timestamp. But first, she brought Tammy through her night with Sidney in more detail. Tammy acknowledged they had driven near the Tilted Kilt on Dec. 17, 2013, but said a lot of restaurants were in that area, including the restaurant where her mother was a waitress.

"Let me ask you this: Was the bitch in hiding on the 17th?"

"I don't know where she was on the 17th. It was the least thing on my mind."

"You rode by her house?"

"No, I didn't ride by her house. I didn't know where Heather lived. Ever."

"And then you went down where Longbeard's is?"

"I don't know what Longbeard's is. I didn't hear that until I was in this courtroom."

"You've heard the testimony, correct?" asked Livesay.

"I've heard a lot of lies in this courtroom."

"Who were you calling when you were in the Walmart parking lot?"

"I was talking to Kevin (the New Jersey musician)."

"And Kevin was the guy that was your boyfriend at the time?"

"He was my friend at the time that I was talking to him. He was not the one I was having sex with."

"The pregnancy test was really for Heather, wasn't it?"

"It was not for Heather. You could listen to the interview," she said, referring to the session with Sgt. Large. "You wouldn't even know we bought it. We told the police what we did so you could get surveillance. And then you decided to twist it and try and trick people. Heather had her period Dec. 9, and I'm pretty sure you know that if you looked at the evidence."

"But you had a period, too, didn't you?"

"I did. I wasn't pregnant until I went to jail. I found out I was pregnant."

"And you know the pregnancy box was in the trash can?"

Tammy smiled. "It wasn't during Sidney's trial."

"But you would admit the testimony here was that the box was in the trash can?

"I agree that witnesses have changed their testimony. Yes, they've lied."

"You left Walmart around 1:21," Livesay continued. "Ten minutes later, a phone call was made to Heather Elvis."

"That's what y'all are saying, but that makes no sense," Tammy said. "I didn't make a pay phone call, and Sidney didn't make a pay phone call. He was forced to tell cops that when they held him against his will."

"It just happens that 10 minutes after you buy a pregnancy test, right up the road from the Walmart, that pay phone called Heather Elvis?"

"What you're trying to trick everyone into believing doesn't make sense," said Tammy. She insisted that the only thing that made sense was for Sidney to call Heather first and then buy the pregnancy test.

"Are you familiar with the clock? How it works?"

"I am."

"Do you know that 1:21 a.m. to 1:33 a.m. is around 10 minutes? Eleven minutes?"

"We've established that Heather received a call," said Tammy. "I'm telling you it wasn't from me and it wasn't from Sidney. Sidney was being held against his will at the police station when he asked for an attorney. They wouldn't let him leave and put force on him and held him. I know when he was persuaded to admit to making a phone call that he was thinking it would send him home."

"And you know that both of y'all's phones when you were calling your boyfriend is pinging by that pay phone?"

"You're talking about an area in a three-block range. Myrtle Beach is little. So if you want to say that it pinged there because of an odd reason, that's you, that's on you. But when we're going from one place over to another place to get gas or whatever, it's the same tower. You have the facts and you're not telling the people what's going on here."

Livesay wrapped up cross-examination about asking about Tammy's claim to have an alibi via Facebook post at 3:35 a.m.

"I have documentation that I was sitting at my computer posting," said Tammy.

"How about at 3:40?"

"I don't think so."

"How about 3:45?"

"I don't know."

"How about 3:50?"

"There's 3:58, I believe."

"How about 3:50?" Livesay repeated.

"No."

"How about 3:55?"

"No."

"So you've got all kinds of documentation showing before the truck went down there?"

"I have documentation for all hours during the night."

"But you just admitted you have nothing showing 3:35?"

"I don't have something showing going on every second of the day. I'm not obsessed with the internet that way."

"Ironically, you have it going on before the truck goes down and after?"

"And during."

"Not during!" Livesay said. "I just asked you. We're going to get that straight. I asked you."

"My son saw me in the hall. I have an alibi witness that you refuse to let testify. I don't agree with the videos. I think they were either made up or it's someone else's vehicle."

"And do you know that you can change the date and time of a post to whatever you want it to be?"

This seemed to surprise Tammy. "I do not know, but you can't change the other stuff."

Livesay showed Tammy a copy of Facebook's directions on how to change a date and time on posts.

"I guess you can change it," said Tammy. "I haven't been on Facebook in over a year."

Livesay ended her cross-examination by noting that the screenshots Tammy brought to court had been taken three days earlier.

After short, follow-up questions on redirect examination, the judge asked McCollum if the defense had any more witnesses.

"No, your honor. At this time, the defense rests."

25.

Nancy Livesay's third summation proved her strongest, her most literary, most personal.

"I remember," she began, "when I was little girl and my mom would read me stories. I'll never forget my favorite one. My mom was reading about the woman who looked into the mirrors. She would say, 'Mirror, mirror on the wall, who is the fairest of them all.' Everything was fine as long she saw her reflection in the mirror."

All that changed when she saw another face in the mirrors.

"This story is a lot the same way," said Livesay of the Heather Elvis case. She held up a photo of Heather. "When she saw this face is when this story began."

What Tammy Moorer cherished, her love of all things Disney, had been turned against her. In Livesay's telling, Tammy was the evil witch. Angry at her husband, obsessed with the younger, more beautiful woman he had an affair with, Tammy sunk into misery, "smoking and drinking," her only escape to eliminate the threat, according to Livesay.

Tammy probably followed Heather, waiting for the perfect opportunity when she'd be alone and vulnerable, said Livesay. That opportunity arrived when Heather's roommate went out of town. They could only have known that because they were probably looking for her and following her, their itinerary that night taking them by the Tilted Kilt and near her apartment.

Within minutes after Stephen Schiraldi dropped her off at home, her cell phone rang: Sidney calling to say he had left his wife and wanted to meet her. He didn't tell her he had bought a pregnancy test. Sidney—humiliated, guilt-ridden, handcuffed-to-the-bed Sidney—became a pawn in Tammy's scheme.

"Tammy has the motive, Sidney has the means," Livesay said. "It takes Sidney to lure her out."

It was to be a confrontation. Sidney had the pregnancy test. Tammy wanted answers. "How do we know who the pregnancy test is for?" asked Livesay. "This phone call tells us how we know. As soon as they leave from Walmart, they go and call her. What couple goes into a Walmart and buys a test for each other and immediately goes out and calls his girlfriend? That test wasn't for Tammy. She hated Sidney. I would suggest this pregnancy test was to find out how bad she hated Heather."

After Sidney talked to her for "four daggone minutes," the action shifts to Peachtree Landing, the surveillance video showing his truck going there. Livesay suggested Heather was eager to meet Sidney.

Phone records showed she went home briefly, where she had taken a pregnancy test—the box was later found in her bathroom—and wanted to give Sidney the news "about whatever that stick shows."

"Let's get real. When a woman takes a pregnancy test, the first person she wants to show is the person she believes is the father," said Livesay. "She was going to show him because she went right to the Landing."

Only when she called Sidney back to arrange the meeting, it was on speaker phone, and Tammy was listening—and recognized her voice, as she later told the sheriff's investigator.

"When Heather is calling at 3:38 from the Landing, his truck was passing that camera on Mill Pond Road," said

Livesay. "She's sitting down there and has no idea what's in store for her."

Tammy claimed to have been at home talking on Facebook about coupons. "No way you get off the phone with your husband to his girlfriend for four minutes, you're worried about coupons," she said.

Which brought the summation to Livesay's observations about Tammy Moore on the witness stand. She said it spoke for itself. "If you are going to interact with me like that, I can only imagine you would interact with a 20-year-old girl who is basically playing grownup," said Livesay.

"We know that in the end of all the fairy tales, something happens to make it right, whether it's for Cinderella or Snow White or whomever," she concluded. "The story never ended with it being wrong, with it being an injustice. In the end, that person always got what they deserve. Today, I'm going to ask you to give Heather what she deserves."

It was a stirring summation—well paced, well structured, wrapped up in a neat little bow just like a Disney movie. Had there been a soundtrack, the music would have swelled up and the audience sent home happy.

For the defense summation, Greg McCollum tried to bring the jury back to what he called reality. "It's interesting that Miss Livesay, who can spin a yarn, would use as an example of Snow White in a fairy tale," he began, "because her case is a fairy tale."

In fact, he argued, the prosecution didn't know what it was. He quoted Helm's opening statement in which he said they didn't know what happened. McCollum told the jury that before becoming a defense attorney, he was a prosecutor who tried more than 100 cases. "Never in my life would I come in and tell you: I don't know what happened," he said, "but it's a big case, so why don't you do something about it. That's not fair to you. We have been in here for two weeks. We have heard 38 witnesses, who proved what?"

He said the prosecution couldn't even prove what it claimed sent the entire alleged kidnapping plot in motion: that Heather was pregnant.

"A box from her pregnancy test in her garbage?" he asked in a mocking tone. "They say they bought it on the 18th at 1:15 in the morning? How did she get it? If they lured her out, and somehow made her urinate on a pregnancy strip, why would the box go back to her house? Does that make any sense?"

Instead, he said, authorities zeroed in on the Moorers, because they didn't have anybody else, ignoring the fact that the couple cooperated—letting police search their home, their truck, their camper—and went looking for evidence that wasn't there.

"They say that Sidney goes to the boat landing to trick her, finagle her, do whatever," he said. "They don't have evidence, like those twist ties. They don't have evidence of duct tape. They don't have any evidence of a hood like they put over a head. They don't have any evidence somebody had a pack of chloroform they could knock them out with. They didn't have anything. It's not there. That's called a lack of evidence."

Had there been an abduction, police should have found something. "Most people fight back," he said. "They kick out windows. They break stuff. They bite people. They scratch people. They do things. There's nothing. The truck is clean as a whistle."

What authorities had, he suggested, was pressure from the public. McCollum managed to sneak in, without having presented any evidence, troubles at the police department, with a "chief of police who's no longer the chief of police, officer no longer with the department, some of them fired, one of them dead, just a mess."

Like the prosecutor, he said, the defense also didn't know what happened to Heather Elvis. But there were danger signs, avenues the police didn't explore in their zeal to nab the Moorers.

"I think it's significant that witnesses testified that she was homeless, she was abused by people, she got bruised, she made up a story about stabbing somebody, she was living with this guy and she was living with that guy, sleeping in her car, living out of her car, sleeping on the couch," he said. "It's not stable. It's terrible. It's awful. She has an awful life."

He urged the jury not to get the wrong impression. "We're not saying that she didn't deserve to live. We're not saying that," he said. "We're saying, 'Look, we don't know what happened to her. She was working at the Tilted Kilt. She was having relationships with a lot of different people. She was in a vulnerable position to have contact with people who might try to harm her.'"

In the end, he told the jury, the defense did not have to prove what happened and did not have to prove that Tammy didn't do anything. Tammy was presumed innocent. The prosecution had to prove guilt beyond a reasonable doubt, and here, he said, it failed.

Grasping his hands in front of him as if in prayer, he said, "Don't feel that outside pressure. You're stronger than that, you're better than that. If you do what you're supposed to do and follow your oath, and you look at the lack of evidence and the contradictions, I'm confident that each and every one of you will reach a unanimous verdict of: Kidnapping, not guilty; conspiracy to kidnap, not guilty. When you do that, whatever occurs in the future, this ordeal, this mistreatment, this horrendous treatment of Tammy Moorer will be over."

The jury was sent home. Deliberations were to begin the next day at 9 a.m.

26.

It wasn't 50 minutes. But it was quick. The jury spent four hours in the deliberation room before delivering a note to the judge around lunchtime on Tuesday, Oct. 23, 2018.

Attorneys and family members assembled in the courtroom. Tammy Moorer took her seat next to her two attorneys. The judge gazed out from the bench with a final message to the spectators before bringing the jury in.

"This has been a long trial, and I know there's a lot of emotions involved in this," he said. "But there will be absolutely no display or outburst or any reaction in regards to what the verdict might be. I tell you this because the jury doesn't want to be here. They didn't volunteer for this job. It's been a tough job for them. If you are unable to contain your emotions, whatever the verdict might be, you need to go ahead and excuse yourself from the courtroom right now."

Nobody left.

"All right, anything from the state before we bring the jury in?"

"No, sir," said Livesay.

"Anything from the defense?"

"No, your honor," said McCollum.

"Let's go ahead and bring the jury in," the judge said.

As the jurors assumed their seats, Tammy sat grim-faced, her three children and mother sitting behind her. Court security officers in bulletproof vests beneath their gray uniform shirts were standing ready around the courtroom. Heather's parents, Terry and Debbi Elvis, huddled with their other daughter.

"Ladies and gentlemen, welcome back," the judge told the jury. "I understand the jury has reached a verdict. Is that correct?

The forewoman said, "Yes sir."

"Have you completed the verdict form?"

"Yes, sir."

"Have you signed it?"

"Yes, sir."

"Can you please hand it to the bailiff?" The bailiff took the verdict form, on a white sheet of paper, and gave it to the judge to review. He gave it to his clerk. Tammy and her lawyers stood. The courtroom was completely quiet.

"The state of South Carolina, the County of Horry vs. Tammy Caison Moorer," the clerk said. "We the jury find the defendant, Tammy Caison Moorer, guilty of kidnapping."

Tammy didn't flinch. Her mother wept softly.

The clerk continued reading: "We, the jury, find the defendant, Tammy Caison Moorer, guilty of conspiracy to kidnap."

The clerk noted the forms were signed by the forewoman. Muffled crying could be heard. Heads turned to the Elvis family. They wept silently. Otherwise, no outbursts. The judge thanked the jury for their service, wrapped up last-minute legal matters, denying the defense's obligatory motion for a new trial, and moved straight to the last order of business.

"Are we ready to go ahead and impose sentence?" asked the judge

Both sides said they were. During a brief lull for attorneys to gather their notes and legal documents, Tammy stood, turned around and embraced her oldest son and daughter together. She patted her daughter's back as if to comfort her.

The judge turned to the defense table. "Any mitigation?"

McCollum, sounding tired and deflated, gave a rote recitation of Tammy's good points borrowed from the bond hearings. "Tammy is a local product there," he said. "She grew up in Horry County, she's a lifelong resident, all of her family is from here as well. Her father is deceased, her mother, Polly, is seated behind her. As your honor has heard in the case, Polly has worked for decades as a server. She's also recorded albums and is a member of the Pentecostal church down there in Socastee. She sang in choir-type settings."

McCollum was rambling, the strain of the trial and the shock of the verdict seemingly catching up with him. He pointed to Tammy's children. He said despite the incarceration of their parents for nearly a year, the kids caught up on their schoolwork and graduated on time.

"That's a testament to her and her resolve and character with those children," he said, bringing it back to Tammy. "She has got no prior criminal history. At the time of her arrest, she was working as a travel agent, doing her passion, which is Walt Disney-type tours."

He noted that she obeyed the rules of her bond. She appeared in court every time she was supposed to.

"Your honor," McCollum said wearily, "clearly, the defense is very disappointed with the outcome. We really thought that the verdict should have been different in this case, and we would ask your honor to show whatever leniency you'd be able to."

"Miss Moorer," the judge asked, "anything you want to say?"

"Yes, sir," she said. "Obviously, I was unhappy with my representation. I wanted different attorneys. I don't think they fought for me. … I never felt comfortable with them, and I never had a way out. I felt like I had to do my own trial. That I'm not an attorney. I don't know how to do these things. And I just don't think I had a fair advantage over any of this."

Done complaining about her lawyers, she said, "I'm a mom to four kids because I have an extra one I'm looking out for. They don't have anybody else. They don't live in this state. They had to leave this state because of harassment. They don't have anybody else to care of them. And they need their mom."

She spoke in a calm, matter-of-fact way, with no emotion. As for the case, she insisted that, "I am Heather's number one advocate. I want to know what happened to Heather, probably just as much as her parents do. I want to know what happened to her. I know I had nothing to do with her disappearance. I've never met her. I've never seen her in person. The truth is in the boxes."

The boxes of documents, evidence and other discovery materials the prosecution turned over to the defense. She said "they"—she didn't say who—"have not even shown me 90 percent of that. They know where Heather is by that discovery. And it has just not been brought to court. I want it brought to court and light. I want to know what happened, too. I feel like I'm begging for my life for something I did not do, for something I didn't have anything to do with. I wish there was just a way to show you everything."

"Thank you, ma'am," the judge said.

The judge then gave an opportunity for Heather's family to speak. Her father, Terry, walked up to the microphone and gave his name in a voice raspy from emotion.

"Mr. Elvis, what would you like to say?"

"Your honor, thank you for allowing me to speak," he said, struggling to get the words out. His wife and younger daughter came up and stood on either side of him.

"My family has gone through hell for over 4½ years. My daughter is still missing to this day. No one seems to want to take the blame for it. We grieve for answers because we don't know how to grieve for our daughter."

He asked the judge to impose the maximum sentence, which would be 30 years for each charge. He asked that Tammy be ordered to serve both terms back to back.

"Kidnapping is not a one-time deal," he said. "It didn't happen one day and the next day it didn't. It's every day, it's every minute, it's every second. This court is not going to fix that by sentencing her to jail, I understand that. The problem still goes on for us every day. I would like to say that I feel for the accused, but I can't. I cannot."

His wife, Debbi, followed him, her remarks tinged with more anger. "I thought what I wanted to say for five years, and it changes every week," she said, then spoke directly of the Moorers. "It wasn't enough what they did. They had to disparage her and shame her in a public eye afterward on social media and then in the community. Then that wasn't enough. They had to do that to our family, attack our family's reputation, talk to the media and say everything they could about the family."

She spoke of threats and bullets left on their vehicle, of a trashcan that got shot up. "We have been through a living hell for the past five years brought on by this family and the people that they have gathered on social media," she said, talking now through tears. "What they did to Heather wasn't enough for them. They keep digging. They won't release our daughter. They took her and they won't let her go. Five years later, they're still holding her hostage. They stole her life and they've ruined ours. There's no sentence you can give until she"—Tammy—"comes forward and lets our daughter go." Now sobbing, she said, "I know that she has children. I feel for them. But she didn't think about her children when she made this decision. She didn't think about anyone else."

The last to speak was Heather's younger sister, Morgan. Crying as her father had, his hand on her back, she said, "As much as I do feel for Tammy Moorer, and as much as I do feel for her children, my sister never got to hold onto her parents and cry and say goodbye." Tammy's cruelty, she said, had no bounds. "Our community as a whole has been broken. My family has fallen apart and will never recover."

From the day after Heather disappeared, the Elvis family has said these words countless times to countless television cameras, and yet now, it sliced through the courtroom, the pain visceral and raw. It contrasted with Tammy's monotone. It was emotionally brutal.

Over the sound of sniffling in the courtroom, the judge filled out some forms, then addressed Tammy again.

"Miss Moorer, you have been found guilty by jury trial on charges of kidnapping and conspiracy to kidnap," he said. "The sentence of the court for each charge is that you be confined to the state Department of Corrections for 30 years. The sentences are to run concurrently. You'll be given credit for any time served thus far."

He looked up at the attorneys.

"Anything further from the state on this matter?"

"No, your honor," said Helms.

"Anything from the defense?"

"No, judge," said McCollum.

Tammy hugged her sobbing mother, then was escorted by two security officers through a brown door at the back of the courtroom and into the lockup.

27.

In the justice system, 10 years doesn't really mean 10 years.

While authorities once suspected him of committing murder, in the eyes of the law, Sidney Moorer was a non-violent offender, having been convicted of only obstruction of justice. That meant that despite being sentenced to a decade in prison, he was first eligible for parole only 17 months later, in March 2019.

No sooner had the Elvis family endured the kidnapping trial of Tammy Moorer than they found themselves, on Nov. 27, 2018, sitting in a conference room in front of a closed-circuit camera pleading with the three members of the South Carolina parole board to keep Sidney locked up longer.

It had been a bumpy month since Tammy Moorer was convicted of kidnapping their daughter Heather and sentenced to 30 years in prison. The day after the sentencing, Heather's father, Terry Elvis, was back in court, this time facing a charge of his own.

On the first day of the trial, Terry confronted defense attorney Casey Brown at a courthouse restroom during a break, yelling, "Hey, you're a lowlife piece of shit!"

Brown walked away. But as Terry followed him, Brown asked a bailiff, "Is he talking to me?"

While it was hardly the worst thing ever hurled at a criminal defense lawyer, Brown said he felt intimidated.

Brown reported it to the judge, who held a hearing. Terry's attorney said Brown had been using a restroom on the side of the courthouse reserved for the Elvis family and supporters. They were supposed to be kept separate from the defense team.

The judge held Terry in contempt and fined him $400. Terry told a TV reporter he was inundated with offers from people to pay it.

Now, five weeks later, Terry; his wife, Debbi; and daughter, Morgan, were giving statements to the parole board. Sidney also appeared via closed-circuit video from the Lee Correctional Institution. He was joined by his older son and daughter. Behind him was Tammy's mother, Polly.

Sidney, now 42 years old, wearing a tan prison jumpsuit, told the parole board that he'd been praying and taking classes.

"I took some welding classes, vocational classes. I work in the dorm every day, cleaning and stuff like that," he said. "Basically, just trying to prepare myself, to better myself as best I could."

A parole board member asked him, "How do you feel about what you did?"

"I know it was wrong. I mean, I'm not going to say I wasn't."

"Would you do it over again?"

He shook his head. "No, sir, definitely not," he said. "I understand what I did was wrong—any crime is not a small crime to me."

"If you understood what you did, why did you do it?"

"Well, I didn't intentionally do it, but I mean, I understand what I did was wrong. I know I did."

He added, "I think if I was given a chance, there would be no issue with me ever again."

In fact, Sidney had a rather large issue hanging over his head. Prosecutors intended to try him again on the kidnapping count, though a trial date had not yet been set. In the meantime, the Elvis family wanted to make sure he stayed in prison.

Terry said, "I don't think he's done his penance in prison yet." Debbi said, "He has not taken responsibility for anything he's done." Morgan said, "I think that it's awfully wrong for him to lie and lie and lie and get to sit at home on Christmas Eve like nothing happened."

Prosecutor Christopher Helms told the board that even though Sidney was up for parole for a non-violent offense, the fact remained that he still was staring down a kidnapping count in a case in which his lies hindered the closure for the Elvis family.

"One of the goals of the prison system is rehabilitation," said Helms. "We have no indication that Mr. Moorer has been rehabilitated. We have no indication that he has any degree of remorse for what he did. Again, I know this is obstruction of justice. But folks, he did not obstruct a shoplifting case. He did not obstruct a grand larceny case. This initially was a homicide investigation that then morphed into kidnapping charges. I would like to remind you those charges are still pending against Mr. Moorer."

By a unanimous vote, the board rejected Sidney's parole bid.

As for Tammy, she was sent to the medium-security Leath Correctional Institution in Greenwood, S.C., where she was working as an assistant to one of the prison administrators.

She was reunited with Sidney in court at a December 2018 hearing, where they faced charges unrelated to the Heather Elvis case. Prosecutors allege the couple committed Medicaid fraud by misrepresenting their income on applications.

Sidney and Tammy stood next to each other. A *Sun News* reporter observed them exchanging hellos and "some passing glances." Otherwise, they didn't talk to each other.

The couple is also together in another matter. They hired a lawyer to file a lawsuit against the Horry County Police Department and other agencies for allegedly violating their civil rights.

Peachtree Landing remains much as it always has been, a lonely place on the side of a river, surrounded by trees and swamp. On the night of Dec. 18, 2018, a crowd gathered to mark the fifth anniversary of Heather Elvis's disappearance.

On the spot next to the boat ramp where she very likely spent her last moments, candles burned.

AFTERWORD

On Tuesday, September 10, 2019, Sidney Moore returned to court to once again face kidnapping and conspiracy charges. It had been three years since a mistrial was declared on those same charges against him. This would in all likelihood be the prosecution's last chance to convict Sidney of the same crime for which his wife Tammy was convicted and sentenced to 30 years in prison.

Heather Elvis had now been missing for nearly six years, though that fact still had to be legally established, with prosecutors for Horry County calling Jessica Adams of the South Carolina Law Enforcement Division. She looked into every database available to the state police, from credit card records to police bookings. "I found nothing related to Heather Elvis anywhere in the United States since 2013," Adams said.

Seeking to avoid a repeat of the other trial, the prosecution then presented powerful new evidence: video from Sidney's own security system showing him, his wife and others scrubbing clean their pickup on December 22, 2013, four days after Heather's disappearance and just before the truck was taken to police headquarters for inspection.

This is the same Ford F150 that Sidney and Tammy had been driving around in the night Heather went missing. The GPS system removed shortly before it was captured by other security cameras driving to and from the Peachtree Landing boat ramp, where Heather's abandoned car would be found.

Tammy was vigorously cleaning the passenger side of the cab. She also was seen with her sister Ashley Caison searching around the yard with one of those mirrors security people use to search under cars. Sidney could be seen burning the towels used to wash the truck.

The truck was so clean that police didn't bother taking DNA samples.

Sidney's defense had no answer to this video. When his sister-in-law Ashley Caison was asked on cross-examination about it. She said she didn't remember what she'd done.

On September 20, the jury spent less than two hours deliberating before finding Sidney guilty of kidnapping and conspiracy to kidnap. Heather's father said he'd be willing to let Sidney go free if Sidney would provide one piece of information. "Just tell us where she is," he said through tears.

"I wish I could give them closure," Sidney replied in court. "Anything I would tell them would be a lie."

With that he was sentenced to 30 years in prison.

For More News About Michael Fleeman,
Signup For Our Newsletter:

http://wbp.bz/newsletter

Word-of-mouth is critical to an author's long-term success. If you appreciated this book please leave a review on the Amazon sales page:

http://wbp.bz/mpda

1.

An hour before sunset, Shaun Ware swung his white work truck right off Goodrick Drive into the Summit Industrial Park, a complex of metal buildings with tall garage doors. It was Sunday, Aug. 17, 2014, a warm summer evening in the high desert. Shadows enveloped the Tehachapi Pass, the mighty turbines in the windmill farm standing still in the light western breeze. Traffic roared by on Highway 58, cars and trucks shuttling between Bakersfield and the Mojave Desert. Every half hour, a long freight train from Burlington Northern Santa Fe Railway would rumble behind the complex.

Arriving for his overnight shift, Shaun pulled his truck up to a space with "BNSF" stenciled on the concrete parking block and immediately felt something was wrong. The metal door to the work area was closed. The day-shift responder, Robert Limon, would have kept it open to ventilate the stuffy garage during the 89-degree afternoon. Robert would have told him if he were out on a service call or making a food run.

Shaun raised the door with a remote opener. Robert's BNSF utility truck was parked next to his personal car, a silver Honda. Shaun walked into the garage along the right side of the truck. He nearly stepped on broken glass that appeared to have come from one of the fluorescent fixtures hanging from the 18-foot ceiling.

To his right, the door to the small office was wide open. That was wrong, too. The office door always stayed closed. The office appeared to have been ransacked. File drawers had been yanked open and papers strewn across the floor. A BNSF-issued Toshiba laptop was missing.

Shaun walked around the front of the work truck, which pointed toward the kitchenette against the back wall. The door of the small refrigerator was flung open. So was the door to the bathroom.

That's when he saw him.

Robert Limon was on the floor, his back slumped against the driver's side tire of the truck.

Shaun kneeled.

"Rob, what happened?" Shaun said. "Wake up, buddy."

Robert had a vacant look on his face, one eye closed, the other half opened. Blood had pooled beneath him. He didn't respond.

Panic gripped Shaun. He called 911 on his cell phone. He told the operator that he had found his coworker on the ground around a lot of blood and that he wasn't moving.

The operator asked if Shaun was willing to try CPR. He said yes. Following the operator's instructions, Shaun pulled Robert down flat on his back. He put his face close to Robert's. There was no breath. The operator asked Shaun to push his hands against Robert's chest to begin compressions.

One push and blood oozed out of Robert's mouth.

The operator told Shaun to get out of the building, now. He did, in a daze. The cell phone still to his ear with the 911 operator on the line, he wandered out to the asphalt parking area.

A man approached—somebody who worked in a neighboring unit—and asked Shaun what was going on.

"I think Rob's dead," Shaun told him.

Then it hit him. Shaun dropped to his knees and his body convulsed. He felt tears coming.

How long he was like this, he couldn't remember. The next thing he knew, he heard cars approaching. Sirens. Lights. He looked up and saw a woman in a sheriff's uniform.

Shaun pointed to the garage and said, "He has two kids."

2.

Two deputies from the Kern County Sheriff's Office fielded the 911 call at 6:46 p.m. for a "male found bleeding and not breathing" at 1582 Goodrick Drive, Tehachapi, Calif. They arrived in separate one-deputy patrol cars. Both had often seen the facility from the 58, but had never been on call there.

Goodrick Drive took them to a cul-de-sac with a driveway leading into the five buildings of the complex. Since it was a Sunday night, all of the garage doors were shut—save for one—and the place empty, except for the man crouched on the pavement.

Kern County Senior Deputy Marcus Moncur got there first. The 10-year veteran cop approached the man, who was shaking but saying nothing. A second, deputy, Anna Alvarez, a rookie patrol officer, arrived in her patrol car. Moncur asked her to stay with the man and talk to him while he checked out the garage 50 yards away.

There, the deputy saw the silver Honda and the white Chevy work pickup with the utility bed. On the ground next to the driver's side door, he spotted a man flat on his back. He was a big, strong man, about 6 feet tall, with a shaved head and tuft of beard on his chin. He wore an orange safety shirt, black tank undershirt, gray pants and black shoes.

Moncur could see that the man had a lump on his eye and blood around his mouth and right cheek. A large pool of blood congealed beneath his head and upper body. His right arm extended from his body as if hailing a cab. The body showed signs of lividity, the purple discoloration caused by blood pooling under gravity at low points in the body after the heart stops. Just behind the man, red spots were splattered on an open refrigerator door. A sign on the wall read: "A culture of commitment to safety to each other."

Moncur radioed for a paramedic and walked carefully out of the garage so as not to step on any evidence. He asked Alvarez to cordon off the area as a crime scene.

Within minutes, an ambulance and a paramedic truck raced into the complex. Two emergency medical technicians took the man's vital signs and ran a field EKG reading. No signs of life. The EMTs called a physician at the Kern Medical Center in Bakersfield, recited their findings.

At 7:06 p.m., the man was officially declared dead. Over the next half hour, phone calls went out to supervisors and investigators, plus crime scene technicians and the coroner. Moncur started a crime-scene log to keep track of what would be a small invasion of law enforcement personnel overnight.

He then waited an hour and a half.

Covering more than 8,000 square miles, Kern County is just smaller than the entire state of New Jersey. But with 880,000 people, it has only a tenth of its population. Kern County is vast and in most places, empty. The rectangular-shaped county is made up of sprawling farmland, rugged mountains and wide swaths of desert.

The closest detective was more than an hour's drive away in the county seat of Bakersfield. Randall Meyer of the robbery homicide division got the call at home from the Kern County Sheriff's Office Communication Center at about 7:30 p.m. A former patrol deputy, training supervisor and investigator in the sex crimes unit, Meyer had been transferred to robbery-homicide six months earlier. He put on a suit and tie and headed east for Tehachapi.

He got to the top of the pass at 8:30 p.m. Pulling off Highway 58, he made his way on side streets to Goodrick Drive to the industrial complex. He flashed his ID, got logged in and was directed to the crime scene through two checkpoints, one at the outer perimeter near the entrance to the facility, the second the taped-off inner perimeter closest to the garage.

Darkness had come to the high desert. At an elevation of more than 4,000 feet, even on this summer night the temperature would plunge more than 40 degrees to the mid-50s. The complex was ablaze with emergency lights and full of cops.

Meyer received a briefing from another Kern County detective, Mitchell Adams, who was in charge of processing the crime scene. Adams had phoned another detective with instructions to seek a search warrant from a night-duty judge. In the meantime, Adams had an evidence tech videotape the exterior of the garage. He walked around to the back of the building, looking for any signs of evidence. Behind the garage, in the hard-parked dirt, he spotted what looked like footprints near the back door. He had the tech photograph those. About 15 feet west of the corner while waking southeast, he found another shoe track, also photographed.

After 90 minutes, Adams had a search warrant and for the first time entered the garage. Adams told Meyer that he followed the same path as Shaun Ware along the right side of the truck, stepping over the glass shattered into a powder. The fixture above was missing one of its two fluorescent bulbs and Adams could see some damage to the metal frame.

On the ground, directly below the fixture, he spotted a bullet. It was mangled from apparently hitting the light fixture. It appeared to be a larger caliber, .44 or .45, from a big, powerful gun.

To his right, through the office door, he could see a television, sofa, desk and office chair, exercise machine, photocopy machine, whiteboard, calendar and two desks against the wall. The bottom desk drawers were open and items, including file folders, had been removed and thrown on the floor. Behind the bookcase on the northwest wall were several binders on the ground that Adams believed had been hastily removed from their previous location. Two cell phones sat on the desk.

Walking around the front of truck, Adams saw the body for the first time, the blood on the face and a bump on the back of the head. Behind the man, red dots from blood spatter were on the doors of the refrigerator.

An evidence technician photographed the interior of the office, the bullet fragment on the ground, the tiny blood spatter on the interior of the refrigerator door, the door of the truck—everything Adams pointed out.

That was the extent of the physical evidence. Beside the footprints, Adams found nothing that a killer or killers would have left behind. An evidence tech dusted for fingerprints, but analysis would take days.

"I immediately started thinking that it was possibly a staged scene," Adams later said in court, repeating what he told Meyer. "In numerous investigations, with burglary and robberies and such, I've never seen items placed as those were and the amount of items."

How the victim died would remain a question mark. The bullet on the ground and the blood on and around the body suggested he was shot. The bump on the head could have come from a blow. An autopsy would sort that out.

No gun or other weapon was found. Nor did they find spent brass ammunition shells, suggesting the shooter used a revolver or picked up the ejected shells from a semi-automatic.

Meyer was led to the "reporting party," Shaun Ware. A burly man with a shaved head, Shaun could have been the victim's brother. Shaun explained that the garage was leased by Burlington Northern Santa Fe Railway as a repair shop.

He and the victim, whom he identified, worked as "rapid responders," going into the field when trains break down, which they had a habit of doing on the Tehachapi Pass.

From the flat San Joaquin Valley, the trains strain up the grade, so steep in one spot that the tracks form a circle, like a spiral staircase, that takes the trains up 77 feet in a mile. Train buffs flock from around the world to see the famed Tehachapi Loop. YouTube is full of scenes of the loop.

Some 20 trains a day labor up the pass, making it one of the busiest stretches of single track in the country and one of the hardest on engines. Metal cracks, hoses blow, wires short circuit. That's when the phone rings in the BNSF garage in Tehachapi. A rapid responder jumps in a truck and races out to the scene of the breakdown, diagnosing the problem and making repairs.

Shaun told the detective the Tehachapi responders work 12-hour shifts. They always work alone. The 7 p.m. to 7 a.m. shift the night before belonged to Shaun, that day's 7 to 7 to Robert Limon.

The last time he'd spoken to Robert was that morning during the 7 a.m. shift change. They talked about Robert's iPad, which was not working. Shaun slept all day before his overnight shift and had no idea what Robert had done during the day shift.

Meyer asked Shaun how well he knew Robert. He said he'd worked with him off and on for about two years. "He was a very friendly guy, very outgoing," Shaun later said in court, repeating what he told Meyer.

Robert was married with two kids and lived in a community called Silver Lakes, in the town of Helendale, in San Bernardino County, about an hour-and-half drive away toward Barstow. Shaun had never known Robert to use drugs or have been involved in any illegal activities. He couldn't think of anybody who'd had an argument with Robert, much less want to harm him.

Then Shaun said something that Meyer found particularly intriguing. Robert did not usually work in Tehachapi. He was based far across the Mojave Desert to the east at Barstow Yard, BNSF's sprawling rail classification yard where rolling stock is changed between engines along a labyrinth of tracks. According to Shaun, Robert was filling in that Sunday for the regular responder, who was either out sick or taking vacation time. Shaun didn't know which employee was out but he knew that Robert had taken the shift at the last minute.

Shaun told him something else: the BNSF work truck in the garage, like all trucks, was equipped with a forward facing camera that activates during accidents. It may have captured something.

When the processing of the scene was complete, the body was released to the coroner's investigator, who put bags over the hands to preserve evidence and pulled the wallet from the victim's back pocket. The driver's license confirmed what Shaun Ware had said. The victim was Robert Limon, age 38, with a home address on Strawberry Lane in Helendale.

The coroner investigator and two other body removal assistants placed the corpse into a blue body bag and sealed it with a tag. Robert Limon—husband, father and railroad worker—was now coroner number C01615-14.

One of the cell phones in the office belonged to Robert. It had several missed phone calls and text messages. The last text came at 8:30 p.m.: "Babe I'm worried about you. Call me. Leanna wants to say goodnight."

Det. Randall Meyer would find out that the text had come from Robert's wife, now widow.

It was never returned.

3.

"Detective, what happened to my husband?"

The woman's voice sounded tired and stressed.

"I do want to give you some information real quick," Det. Randall Meyer told her, but then the cell reception got fuzzy, and she told him to call her landline. "This is Detective Meyer again," he told her when he called back. "I just have some questions for you, and then we'll talk a little bit about what's going on."

It was 1:30 a.m. when Det. Meyer called Sabrina Limon. She was at home in Silver Lakes. In the background, Meyer could hear adults talking and the voices of children. The house on Strawberry Lane was full of relatives, friends and the two Limon children, son Robbie, 11, and daughter Leanna, 8. Death draws a crowd.

He called her after what could only have been the worst night of her life. When Sabrina's husband didn't come home, didn't answer his phone and didn't reply to her texts, she called her older sister, Julie Cordova, and their parents. They all lived in Silver Lakes and came over immediately—Julie accompanied by her husband and one of her two sons and his wife.

Then at about 8:30 p.m., a white BNSF Jeep pulled up to the house. Two men from the railroad came to the house to tell Sabrina that her husband had died at work in Tehachapi. All they knew was that it appeared to be an injury to his head. Police were investigating.

Julie watched as her sister collapsed on the porch in tears. Robbie and Leanna started crying.

Julie's husband demanded more information, but they said they didn't know anything more. Her husband wasn't so sure. He once worked for BNSF—he was the one who had helped Robert get hired there back in 2000. Then he suffered an injury on the job. The Cordovas tangled over a settlement. "They did not take care of him," Julie later claimed. Her husband told them he wanted to drive to Tehachapi and find out for himself what was going on. The railroad men urged him to stay away and not interfere with police. He reluctantly agreed.

Julie started making phone calls.

"Julie called me probably about 10:30 in the evening," Robert Limon's sister, Lydia Marrero, recalled in an interview. "She had told me there had been a terrible accident and my brother was gone. I said: 'What happened to my brother?' And she couldn't tell me. The next thing, I just lost it."

All Julie knew was that Robert had died at work. Lydia, who lives with her husband, Reyes, in the San Bernardino Valley community of Rialto, wanted to make the 120-mile drive to Tehachapi that night, but Julie talked her out of it.

"She said we probably couldn't talk to anybody there, so we waited until the next morning."

After 1 a.m. the Kern County coroner's office called the house and an investigator officially notified Sabrina that her husband was dead. The investigator had little more information than the railroad men. Sabrina heard her say something about Robert still having his wallet.

Then Sabrina's cell phone rang. It was Det. Meyer. She ended the call with the coroner investigator and asked Meyer to call her back.

"Your husband," Meyer said, "his first name was Robert, correct?"

"Robert, yeah."

"What time did he leave to go to work yesterday?"

"He leaves about 5 o'clock."

"In the morning?"

"Uh-huh."

"And why was he coming to work here in Tehachapi?"

"He's a responder. He relieves when guys go on vacation."

"Does he normally work somewhere else?"

"He's a car inspector in Barstow Yard."

"Do you know why he was working over here yesterday?"

"He got called. A guy asked if he could work. One of the guys needed him to cover. I'm not sure why."

"What's his normal shift he works in Barstow?"

"He has Thursday, Fridays off. He works 7 to 3 p.m. in Barstow Yard."

"From what you're aware, he was coming in to cover for somebody here in Tehachapi? He left Sunday morning at 5 a.m.?"

"Yes."

Meyer would later find out that Robert was filling in for a responder named Cory Hamilton. A railroad employee for only a year, Cory had met Robert when Cory was hired in the fall of 2013. He knew Robert only through work, chatting during shift changes. More important, Cory was the responder who had been scheduled to work that Sunday day shift. With family visiting from out of town, Cory took sick days for that Saturday and Sunday. Another fill-in employee, John Justus, covered the Saturday shift, but couldn't do Sunday. It was Justus who got in touch with Robert Limon on Saturday and arranged for him to go to Tehachapi on Sunday.

"Did you speak to him in the morning before he left?" Meyer asked Sabrina.

"I hugged him goodbye. He always wakes me up before he leaves for work."

"Did you have a chance to talk to him throughout the day yesterday?"

"I talked to him a little after 1. And then I talked to him again. He was on a call and he said he was stuck on a train and he said it was—he called it 'A Million Dollar Train.' It was a UPS train where they carry, they call—how did he tell me?—he called it a hot train. He said he was getting it going and he said he got a sandwich and he just had to pick it up. … I talked to him and he was back in the shop."

As Sabrina was starting to ramble, Meyer said, "Let's back up a little bit. When you talked to him at 1 p.m., is that when he said he was working on the train?"

"Uh-huh."

"And he got lunch? Where did he go to lunch at?"

"He ordered a sandwich from a bakery. He has a favorite place he always goes to."

"And do you know the name of that place?"

"It's just, like, the only one in town. He always gets a tuna melt, he tells me about it."

"So you talked to him at 1 o'clock. How long was your conversation?"

"Not long. I told him I would call him back."

She recalled that he called her cell phone, reaching her shortly after she had come out of church, which would have been around 1:30 p.m.

"I called him back from the landline and talked to him for a little bit," Sabrina said. "He said he was tired and he said he was going back to the shop. He said he had been chasing trains. He was going to go back and take a nap."

"What time was that call?"

"I'm going to say about 2:30, about 2 maybe. I have my girlfriend here. She said her husband talked to him about 1:30. I talked to his mom, and his mom talked to him today. I asked her what time it was and I can't remember what she told me."

"About 2:30, you talked to him and he said he was little bit tired and heading back to the shop. And you said you also talked to him while he was at the shop, correct?"

"He was at the shop. I said, 'Lay down and take it easy,' and then usually, he'll call me after he wakes up. But I got busy around here. And I called him about probably about 4:30, maybe even closer to 5, and I was going to go to my mom's and see her. And I called him, and he didn't answer. I also sent him a text to say call me on my cell phone; I'm going to go over and see my mom."

Her parents also lived in Silver Lakes. She was visiting her mother to see how she was doing while recovering from a broken hip.

"I stayed over there until about 6, little after 6," Sabrina said, "and the kids and I came home. And our kids are supposed to start school tomorrow. So I was getting them ready. I called him on the way home on my cell phone. No answer. And then called him again from the home line. No answer. And then I thought he must be on call."

She kept calling Robert because it was getting later and the children would be going to sleep soon to rest up for school.

"Our daughter wanted to talk to him, she started saying, 'Why isn't Daddy answering?'" said Sabrina, who told her daughter he was probably on a repair call. "Then it got closer to 7, and no answer. That was weird, because he'll always call me on his way home. So I just started calling him after that, 7, after 7, 7:30 until it was 8 o'clock. I figured, I was worried about him. I sent him a text. I said call me. Leanna wants to say goodnight to you and I never ..." Her voice trailed off.

Meyer asked, "At what point in time did you hear something from someone?"

It was when the two railroad supervisors came to the house. "I was looking out the window, and they pulled up in a white Jeep," said Sabrina. She then began crying. It was two supervisors from BNSF railroad who came to her house between 8 and 8:30 p.m. They told her only that Robert was dead and that he had a head injury. They said nothing about him being killed, and for much of the night, Sabrina would say, she assumed that Robert had suffered an accident.

Meyer now made it clear that was not the case.

"As far as Robert goes," asked Meyer, "do you know of him having any trouble with anybody?"

"Never."

"Never?"

"Never. Everybody loves Robert."

"Everything going pretty normal with your guys' relationship? There are no issues or anything like that?"

"No, I love him so much."

"There was nobody you can think of that might have been upset with him?"

"No."

"How about his coworkers? How does he get along with his coworkers?"

"Great. Everybody loves Robert," said Sabrina. "Everybody."

"He had never told anybody that he had any issues with coworkers at all whatsoever?"

"No."

Meyer turned to the detective. "Anything you can think of, Detective Robins?"

He said nothing.

"Right now, Sabrina, we're at the very preliminary stages of this whole investigation," Meyer explained. "We don't have a lot of information right now."

"What happened?" Sabrina asked in a pleading tone. "What happened to him?"

"That's it," said Meyer. "We don't know. We don't really have any information yet. We're still working on it right now."

"Where was he? What happened? Did they take his car? She said they didn't take his wallet," said Sabrina, referring to the coroner investigator. "Like, why?"

"Obviously, I can't answer that stuff," said Meyer. He changed the subject. "What type of cell phone does he have?"

"Nothing fancy, but maybe like a 'droid."

She gave him his cell number. "Did you find his phone?"

"I think we did find the phone," said Meyer. It was one of the two phones recovered from the office. "We don't really have a lot of info to go on. We're working on the scene right now. I'm actually away from the scene. ... So I don't even know what's going on yet. What we're going to do, when we're done here, we'll basically do a detective briefing and get everybody up to speed. When I find more information, I'll give you a call and let you know."

"Please," she pleaded, "because I want to know. I want to know. I don't understand. I just don't understand. I don't understand. My brain is not putting this together at all. It isn't even possible. I don't understand. I just want to know what happened. I don't understand. I just want to know."

"As soon as I find out some information, I'll let you know."

"Thank you so much."

"We are working our best right now.

"Thank you."

"I'll call you when I get more information."

"Thank you."

"You have my phone number, call if you ha—"

Sabrina asked: "And you're a detective?"

"Yes," he said.

"Detective Meyer?"

"With the Kern County Sheriff's Office."

"Okay, thank you so much."

The call ended 2:14 a.m. and Meyer would later say that it went about the way he expected. His experience in patrol and sex crimes had him speaking to many people under similar traumatic circumstances. He investigated dead baby cases. And nothing in Sabrina's demeanor raised red flags. She struck him as a suitably upset and confused woman who had no idea what she was going do next for the rest of her life.

Meyer had been calling from a management office at the industrial complex. He had barely seen the crime scene. His ignorance about the circumstances of Rob's death was not invented, though he'd invent plenty before it was over.

One of the investigators had tracked down the landlord and asked if the facility had any surveillance cameras. There were several, in fact, including one at the entrance on Goodrick Drive pointed toward the garage where Robert was killed.

The next day, Meyer would see that footage. Meyer hoped for the best. Unless a witness materialized, it was all he would have to go on.

4.

Later that Monday morning, Sabrina got another visitor from the railroad. Daniel Flatten Jr., the general director of claims for the Burlington Northern Santa Fe Railway, is based in Fort Worth, Texas. By sunrise, Flatten was at the front door with a folder full of paperwork.

Railroad employees don't have Social Security benefits or workers compensation. If injured or killed on the job, they and their families get money from BNSF's own insurance and from a pool of money from the Railroad Retirement Board, an agency established in the 1930s.

Flatten was there to hand deliver the BNSF railroad benefits. Sitting at the kitchen table with Sabrina and her sister, Flatten explained to her the covered details of the insurance, retirement plan and the company 401(k). He also made arrangements to return whatever personal property of Robert's the police had not seized and to make sure Sabrina got Robert's last paycheck. He said the company would also pay funeral expenses up to $15,000.

It was a short meeting and nothing was decided. He gave her his business card and left. The visit seemed to rankle Julie, still bitter over her husband's experience with BNSF. "He was out there the very next day after Rob passed away," said Julie, "and Brina couldn't process it."

Flatten would later say he didn't remember how it came to be, in his words, he simply "showed up" at the Limon's house. Though there was the matter of money. The railroad stood to lose a bundle off of Robert's death. In addition to the usual injury and death benefits, Sabrina could seek an additional direct settlement. For workers who are maimed or die on the job in accidents, the settlements can reach into the millions of dollars.

The Limon case was uncharted territory. Flatten had never handled a case in which a worker was murdered while on the clock. Depending on what police found, this one could be a record payout.

Over the next two months, Flatten kept in touch by phone, sometimes speaking to Sabrina, but mostly dealing with Julie. "I would tell her, 'Brina you have to take care of these kids and yourself,' " Julie said. "It was unsafe where Robert was."

Working all night in remote garages like the Tehachapi shops, some BNSF workers were rumored to carry handguns, in violation of company policy. Their calls took them into wild country at all hours. Robert once told his wife about encountering a bear during a call. He said the Tehachapi area was considered particularly dangerous because so many trains broke down around the Loop, leaving them vulnerable to old-fashioned train robbers seeking valuable cargo.

Within weeks, Flatten broached the subject of a settlement with Sabrina. BNSF had classified Robert as a "high wage earner" whose extra pay for doing relief work put his salary at more than $100,000. Had he worked another 20 years until retirement, he would have made $2 million—a number that would be a logical starting point in settlement talks with BNFS.

It was one of the hallmarks of this case that at critical junctures, Sabrina declined to seek the advice of a lawyer. Early on, BNSF abruptly canceled health insurance for Sabrina and the children, an apparent mistake that Julie worked out on her own. The only advice Sabrina received outside her family came from representatives of the railroad union.

According to Julie, Robert and Sabrina were never tightfisted with money—they loaned Julie and her husband money, voicing no expectations that it would have to be repaid. They also helped cover the student loans for Julie's son. It was Julie who rifled through Sabrina's financial papers and found that Robert had a life insurance policy with a $300,000 payout. Sabrina had said nothing about it. "I was really on her about it," she recalled. "I was so concerned that the kids would be taken care of."

In phone calls from Texas, Flatten went over the settlement process with Sabrina and her sister, but urged them to give BNSF more time. Robert's death was still under investigation by both the Kern County Sheriff's Office and the railroad's in-house police department. Its investigators were working closely with the sheriff's detectives, interviewing witnesses and reviewing records. At least twice, Flatten recalled, he told Sabrina, "We needed to pump the brakes and allow the process to work."

The work was going slowly. From the police standpoint, the whole thing seemed stuck in neutral. Police had no witnesses, little evidence save for a single bullet and some faint shoeprints beside the BNSF building and no apparent motive. Detectives couldn't find anybody who had a bad word to say about Robert. He was financially secure, had no known substance abuse issues, no pending litigation and had not so much as raised his voice at any anyone who police could find. Obviously, a bear didn't kill him.

From a BNSF coworker, Meyer confirmed Sabrina's account that her husband had gone on a service call at around 1 p.m. Robert Garnas, a road foreman based in Bakersfield, met Robert Limon at a train breakdown at a place called Cable Cross Over Station, a few miles west of the Tehachapi garage. They diagnosed the source of the problem—the dynamic brakes on a locomotive—and got to work. Within an hour, the train was up and rolling. The men talked shop. They both knew the new terminal manager in Bakersfield, a guy who had previously "worked up on the hill," as Tehachapi was known, but who now seemed to enjoy life in the city. Robert Garnas liked Robert Limon— nearly everybody did, a big teddy bear of a man. "He always seemed very happy, a big smile," Robert Garnas would say.

The state of the early part of investigation was reflected in the first news accounts. "Helendale Man Found Dead at BNSF Yard," read the headline in the Daily Press based in Victorville, 15 miles south of Helendale. The story appeared on Tuesday, Aug. 19, two days after Robert's body was found, and provided scant details. It said deputies were investigating the murder of BNSF employee Robert Limon, 38, of Helendale, who was found "unconscious" with "obvious signs" of trauma to his upper body, at 6:46 p.m. that previous Sunday in a BNSF maintenance facility in Tehachapi.

Kern County Sheriff's spokesman Ray Pruitt said no arrests had been made and detectives had no possible suspects. "One of the potential motives we're looking at is that he interrupted a burglary or a theft in progress on the property. That's a possible scenario that we're certainly looking at," he said. "There's somebody out there in the community that committed this crime, and we want to identify that person as soon as we can and get that person into custody. This is obviously a very high priority case, and it's a case that we want to solve."

To juice the investigation, BNSF offered a $100,000 reward for information leading to the arrest and conviction of the killer. "Mr. Limon was a valued BNSF employee for 13 years and all those who worked with him are shocked by this tragedy," BNSF said in a statement. "BNSF Railway extends its deepest condolences to his family and friends. … BNSF Police are working closely with the Kern County Sheriff's Office to investigate this senseless crime and ensure the security of BNSF's employees at this location." BNSF spokeswoman Lena Kent told Bakersfield TV station KBAK that Limon was liked and respected. "Everyone is shocked," Kent said. "It's really devastated our community."

The Sheriff's Office then revealed one of the few breaks in the case. As Randall Meyer was talking to Sabrina Limon, an evidence tech was downloading the security video from the five cameras at the Summit Industrial Complex. Most of the footage showed nothing on this lazy Sunday.

But the entrance-mounted camera captured a person, probably a man, wearing bulky clothes and carrying a dark bag. The hunched-over figure was limping left past some trees in the direction of the BNSF garage at 5:21 p.m. Eighteen minutes later, at 5:39 p.m., the person could be seen limping back the opposite way.

The face was too far from the camera to be seen and none of Robert's coworkers or other tenants in the complex recognized the person. So two days after the murder, Det. Meyer released the video to the media and posted it on the Kern County Sheriff's Office YouTube page.

A press release gave Meyer's phone number as well as the number and texting information for the Secret Witness anonymous tip line. That night, the video was all over the Bakersfield and Los Angeles news stations and posted on the websites of the local newspapers. "Hopefully, somebody in the community will recognize the person of interest and we can talk to that person," Pruitt told the media. "Or, somebody will hear something, or has some information that points us in the right direction."

The next day, Meyer would have even more information with which to work. On the morning of Aug. 20, 2014, the remains of Robert Limon arrived in a pouch at the lab of Dr. Robert Whitmore, a forensic pathologist working under contract for the Kern County Sheriff–Coroner, at his offices in Bakersfield down the street from a Home Depot and Walmart.

A graduate of the St. Louis University School of Medicine, Whitmore toyed with psychiatry before changing his specialty to anatomic pathology. After a residency in New York, he got a fellowship with the San Diego County medical examiner's office. He's also a regular doctor, licensed to practice medicine on the living in California and Florida. But on this day, his patient was no longer among the living.

The ID tag was cut and the bag opened, revealing a shrouded corpse; the body had been wrapped in three white sheets at the crime scene. A small group would witness the external and internal examinations: two autopsy aides to assist Whitmore, two evidence technicians shooting photographs and bagging evidence, and one of the sheriff's investigators, Deputy David Hubbard, who took notes.

The removal of the sheets showed that Robert's body was still wearing an orange safety shirt, black tank top undershirt, gray pants, gray boxer briefs, black belt, black socks and black shoes. The clothing was removed and stored for inspection, as were the sterile white evidence-preservation bags that had been placed on his hands at the scene. From Robert's right rear pocket, Whitmore found a note that "appeared to be a note left for him regarding his work." Apparently innocuous, the note warranted no other mention.

The body was photographed clothed and nude, then weighed and measured. At death, Robert was 201 pounds and 5-foot-11½ inches.

As Whitmore examined the outside of the body for trauma and signs of medical procedures, he recited his findings into a handheld Dictaphone and made sketches. He swabbed both hands with sterile wipes for possible DNA evidence and clipped the fingernails. He then sliced open the body for the internal examination, removing each organ one by one, weighing them, looking for evidence of disease or injury and taking tissue samples, before returning the organs to the body cavity. Although lab tests would still be conducted, it appeared that Robert was a perfectly healthy 38-year-old man at the time of death.

http://wbp.bz/boda

Chapter 1: CAROL DENISE SPINKS

The body of a 14-year-old Southeast girl was found yesterday 500 yards south of the Suitland Parkway, near US Route 295, police said. Police said the victim,

identified as Carol Denise Spinks, 1058 Wahler Pl. EW
was discovered about 2:46 p.m. by an 11-year-old boy.
The girl was pronounced dead at 3:15 p.m.
in the DC morgue. Police said the cause
of death has not been determined.
—*The Washington Post*, May 2, 1971

Our nation's capital has always been an anomaly of cities
in the United States. Every other city in the nation resides
within a state. Washington DC has been carved out of
Virginia and Maryland, an urban island of sorts that was at
one time a worthless swampland. It sits astride the border of
northern and southern states, struggling with where it best
belongs.

In the 1970s, the biggest employer in the District was the
federal government. It was what drew a lot of families to the
city, in an era where government employment was seen as
an honored occupation. The District of Colombia residents
still do not have elected senators representing them, and
their vote has only been included in the Electoral College
since 1961. The founding fathers feared that making it a state
would be disruptive to government, and DC has wallowed
in that decision ever since. Even their current license plates
defiantly reads, "Taxation Without Representation."

DC is managed by a mix of local officials with overbearing
influence by the federal government. It is a complex city,
not just because of its strange street layout (courtesy of
the Freemasons) but even how peace is maintained. There
are twelve different police forces currently in the city -
ranging from the Park Police to the Washington National
Cathedral Police to the Secret Service and the Washington
DC Metropolitan Police Department (MPD). In 1971 the
number was even higher, closer to twenty. To an outsider,
it seems strange but to those who live in the city, these are

indicative of the strange status that the city shares as the nation's capital.

By the late 1960s the city was becoming more divided among the lines of prosperity and race. Two-thirds of the city's population was black while at the same time 80 percent of the police force was white. The poorer neighborhoods in the southern parts of the city were populated almost entirely by black families. DC public schools had 92 percent black students; only one out of every three freshmen students in the DC public school system was expected to graduate high school. The divides in the city were deep and self-sustaining. In many respects it was a nuclear reactor, kept in a delicate balance to prevent it from going critical.

The control rods in that nuclear reactor were pulled on April 4, 1968, when Martin Luther King Jr. was assassinated. The black community, long frustrated by the inequalities in the city, turned to violence and vandalism to vent their anger. It started at U Street and 14th Street – the area known as the Black Broadway, spilling down the U Street Corridor. Fires were set and when first responders tried to intervene, they were attacked. Riots sprung up in Logan Circle, Chinatown, and spread to the Capitol Hill neighborhood. The rioting continued for four days, and eventually 13,000 troops from Fort Myer and Fort Meade moved into the city to restore a sense of calm...the most military in the city since the Civil War. The damage from the riots was staggering - at least $175 million in today's dollars. Close to a thousand businesses were damaged, including half of the city's 383 liquor stores. Almost 700 homes and apartments were burned. Police arrested 7,600 adults and juveniles on riot-related charges; thirteen people were killed in the skirmishes between police and rioters. In the end, the underlying problems that had led to the riots had not been resolved by 1971. The burned-out neighborhoods were like ugly scars on the city, charred reminders of the frustration felt by the majority of the population.

The day before the family of Carol Spinks lives changed forever, 500,000 protestors marched down Pennsylvania Avenue in the largest anti-war demonstration. April 24, 1971, was the start of a two weeklong demonstration opposing the Vietnam War that eventually shut down the US government. The protestors called themselves the "Mayday Tribe" with a mission to stop the government if the government wouldn't stop the War. Participants' goal was to nonviolently block traffic and bridges so that government officials wouldn't be able to get into office. The Nixon Administration had most of the protestors blocking traffic arrested before they even got into position using not only police force, but military force as well. It proved to be the largest of the anti-Vietnam war protests to ever hit the city.

The next day, on an unusually warm Sunday evening, Carol Denise Spinks ran into her mother just outside of the 7-Eleven about a half mile from their apartment building. Allenteen Spinks spotted her 13-year-old daughter before she entered the store. She reprimanded her for being out of the house and to return home immediately. It would be the last time Carol would be seen by her mother.

Carol was a typical seventh grader at Johnson Junior High School. She had seven siblings, including an identical twin sister named Carolyn. She was known as the shy and more insecure twin, as Carolyn was much more outgoing, but loved to show off her hula hooping skills. Her passion was jumping double-dutch jump rope, and she loved playing jacks with her siblings. She shared an apartment off Wahler Place with her siblings and her mother, Allenteen. Her older sister, 24-year-old Valerie, lived in the same apartment building and just across the hall from the rest of the family.

Wahler Place is located within the Congress Heights neighborhood of DC, nestled in the hills off the coast of the Anacostia River. After 1954 integration of schools, the number of white families living within Congress Heights rapidly declined. Congress Heights was previously closed to African American families due to segregation.

On April 25, 1971, Valerie asked Carol to go to the 7-Eleven store just seven blocks away to purchase five TV dinners, bread, and soda. Allenteen had strict rules for her children when she wasn't at home; they were not allowed to leave the apartment while she was visiting her aunt in Brentwood, Maryland. Carol decided to take the risk of getting in trouble and took a five-dollar bill to the store.

Carol walked the seven blocks down Wheeler Road, which happened to cross over into the Maryland state line. After running into her mother at the store, Carol was presumed to be heading home. Three hours ticked by without Carol returning to the apartment. The family began to worry and started to call neighbors and friends to ask if anyone had seen Carol. A phone call was made to the 7-Eleven, and the assistant manager said Carol had purchased the TV dinners and left the store at 7:40 p.m. Allenteen reported Carol missing to the Metropolitan Police Station's Seventh District.

In 1971, law enforcement treated missing children's cases differently than today. The police didn't take immediate action. There were no Amber Alerts, no contacting the news media to show pictures. Unless the child was missing for more than twenty-four hours, the police simply noted the call in a log. Chances are, sooner or later, the missing kid would simply return home.

A few witnesses had reported seeing Carol after leaving the store. A fourteen-year-old witness, on the way to the 7-Eleven with her own mother and sister, recalled passing Spinks on the sidewalk carrying a grocery bag. Another witness, Sicilia Diggs, reported seeing two black men jump from a blue car and snatch Carol off Wheeler Road. Diggs claimed that Carol was walking with her friend, Deborah Harrison, at the time and that the other girl had run away when Carol was abducted. Days later, after Carol's body had been found, Deborah Harrison was located and interviewed by police; she admitted to walking with Carol on the night she disappeared but denied watching her get abducted. Deborah also reported that she started receiving several threatening phone calls beginning the day after Carol disappeared indicating that she could be next.

Six agonizing days passed after Carol disappeared before a major break in her missing person's case. On Saturday, May 1, 1971, at 2:46 p.m. an 11-year-old boy wandered away from his friends while playing near the Suitland Parkway in Southeast D.C. Fifteen feet down a grassy embankment on the north bound lanes of Route 295, about 200 yards south of the Suitland Parkway near the Naval Research Lab lay the body of Carol Spinks. According to the FBI report, "The recovery site was along the northbound lanes of the highway was in the rear of the St. Elizabeths Hospital complex. The boy and his friends stopped a traffic officer passing by on Interstate 295 to report the body."

Detective Romaine Jenkins was working in the homicide unit at DC Police Headquarters when a call came in that a body had been found on busy Interstate 295. Detectives John Moriarty and Roy Lamb were dispatched to the scene. Jenkins' supervisor assigned the 28-year-old detective along with two others to interview Spinks' neighbors and relatives. Just as Jenkins was about to head out, the district commander sent her to patrol the streets to help with Vietnam War protestors instead. The young dead girl was not the most pressing thing that the Washington MPD was coping with at the time.

The first officers on the scene were Captain Ellis and Lieutenant Like in Cruiser 219, joined a few minutes later by sergeants Ropel and Mussomele. Once they confirmed that they did, indeed, have a dead body alongside the highway, they called in Detective Sergeant Moriarty of the Homicide Squad along with Mr. Rayford of the Coroner's

Office. Checks were made for missing children reports, and Carol Spinks was at the top of the Washington MPD's list.

Investigators at the scene where her body was found discovered that Carol was clothed in the same clothes in which she had disappeared six days earlier: a red sweater, blue gym shorts, and brown socks. Her size 8 and half blue tennis shoes were missing. Per the FBI report, "When found, the decedent was laying in a face down position, however the body was turned over by an on-looker prior to photographing by the police." As such, the crime scene had already been contaminated.

Her body was taken to the District of Colombia Coroner's Office for an autopsy. According to the medical examiner, she had signs of sexual molestation and abrasions to her hands and face. She had crescent-shaped marks on the left side of her neck, suggesting a ligature may have been used or perhaps these were fingernail impressions from her killer. Her nose was bloodied, and her lower lip was split open. She had been repeatedly sodomized.

The medical examiner estimated her death occurred two to three days prior to the discovery of her body, meaning she had been kept alive for three days before she was killed. The contents of her stomach included some type of citrus fruit, leading to the belief that she had been fed by her killer in the few days she had been kept alive. She had not been simply kidnapped and killed; she had been held prisoner. It should have been a clue, a hint, of the monster that the authorities were going to be up against.

Her official cause of death was asphyxia due to manual strangulation. Forensic examination showed Negroid hairs, unlike her own, on her shorts, sweater, underwear, and hair barrette. Synthetic green fibers were found on her shorts and inside her underwear. Blood was found under her fingernails, but the amount was too small for any conclusive blood-type testing or grouping. It told investigators that she had fought with her attacker. No semen was found anywhere on her body or clothing.

Police began an investigation into the abduction and murder of the petite girl. "Carol would never get into a car with strangers," stated Gloria Dent, a school counselor who worked with Carol.

To this day, Carol's twin sister remembers the day three detectives knocked on the door to inform the family of her death. Allenteen let out a bloodcurdling scream when she learned of her young daughter's fate. The Spinks family's agony was just the start, the beginning. No one knew that her death was the first link in a chain of victims that would terrorize and paralyze the nation's capital.

http://wbp.bz/tantamounta

PLAYING
DEAD

A MEMOIR OF TERROR AND SURVIVAL

"Engaging, powerful, and ultimately shocking story."
–LUNDY BANCROFT, author of *WHY DOES HE DO THAT?*

MONIQUE FAISON ROSS
WITH GARY M. KREBS

PLAYING DEAD by MONIQUE FAISON ROSS

Monique, the daughter of San Diego Charger's football great Earl Faison, married her high school sweetheart soon after she discovered she was pregnant with his child. Her relationship with Chris was shaky from the start, but turned tumultuous as he became verbally and physically abusive. When she could no longer put up with the abuse, she left him with their children. That was when the stalking and genuine threats began. Nothing stopped him—not protection injunctions, police warnings, or even arrests. One fateful Monday morning, Chris kidnapped Monique in front of her children and drove off on a nightmarish car ride that involved car crashes and rape. He mercilessly beat her on the head with a shovel and abandoned her brutalized body in the woods in the rain. He left, presuming she was dead… but was she?

"Monique Faison Ross shares with us her engaging, powerful, and ultimately shocking story of brutal intimate violence. Her survival, her strength, and her wisdom are an inspiration and a lesson to us all. This is a not-to-be-missed opportunity to hear what the targets of domestic violence are trying to tell us, told in a way that will keep you turning the pages."—**Lundy Bancroft, author of Why Does He Do That? and The Joyous Recovery**

http://wbp.bz/playingdeada

More True Crime You'll Love From WildBlue Press

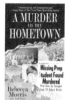

A MURDER IN MY HOMETOWN by Rebecca Morris

Nearly 50 years after the murder of seventeen year old Dick Kitchel, Rebecca Morris returned to her hometown to write about how the murder changed a town, a school, and the lives of his friends.

wbp.bz/hometowna

THE BEAST I LOVED by Robert Davidson

Robert Davidson again demonstrates that he is a master of psychological horror in this riveting and hypnotic story ... I was so enthralled that I finished the book in a single sitting."—James Byron Huggins, International Bestselling Author of The Reckoning

wbp.bz/tbila

BULLIED TO DEATH by Judith A. Yates

On September 5, 2015, in a public park in LaVergne, Tennessee, fourteen-year-old Sherokee Harriman drove a kitchen knife into her stomach as other teens watched in horror. Despite attempts to save her, the girl died, and the coroner ruled it a "suicide." But was it? Or was it a crime perpetuated by other teens who had bullied her?

wbp.bz/btda

SUMMARY EXECUTION by Michael Withey

"An incredible true story that reads like an international crime thriller peopled with assassins, political activists, shady FBI informants, murdered witnesses, a tenacious attorney, and a murderous foreign dictator."—Steve Jackson, New York Times bestselling author of NO STONE UNTURNED

wbp.bz/sea

Made in the USA
Monee, IL
26 August 2022

12527851R00154